D1278561

LIGHTHOUSES SERIES

Mid-Atlantic

LIGHTHOUSES

HUDSON RIVER *to* CHESAPEAKE BAY

Second Edition

PHOTOGRAPHS BY BRUCE ROBERTS
TEXT BY RAY JONES

INSIDERS' GUIDE®

GUILFORD, CONNECTICUT
AN IMPRINT OF THE GLOBE PEQUOT PRESS

3 1267 13936 4010

Fresnel lenses, like this one in Portsmouth, Virginia, use polished glass prisms to concentrate light into a beam of exceptional brillance.

To buy books in quantity for corporate use or incentives, call **(800) 962–0973, ext. 4551,** or e-mail **premiums@GlobePequot.com.**

INSIDERS' GUIDE ®

Copyright © 1989, 1990, 1994, 1995, 1996, 2006 by Bruce Roberts and Ray Jones

All rights reserved. No part of this book may be reproduced or transmitted in any form by any means, electronic or mechanical, including photocopying and recording, or by any information storage and retrieval system, except as may be expressly permitted by the 1976 Copyright Act or by the publisher. Requests for permission should be made in writing to The Globe Pequot Press, P.O. Box 480, Guilford, CT 06437.

Insiders' Guide is a registered trademark of The Globe Pequot Press.

All photographs, unless otherwise credited, are by Bruce Roberts.
Maps are by M.A. Dubé © The Globe Pequot Press.

Library of Congress Cataloging-in-Publication Data is available.

ISBN 0-7627-3042-0

Printed in China
Second Edition/First Printing

To the men and women of the old United States Lighthouse Service. They transformed the darkness along the shore into points of light that gave America the best-lighted coastline in the world.
—*Bruce Roberts*

To the children of America's lighthouse keepers.
—*Ray Jones*

Turkey Point Light, Elk Neck, Maryland. (© Mark Riddick/New Light Photography)

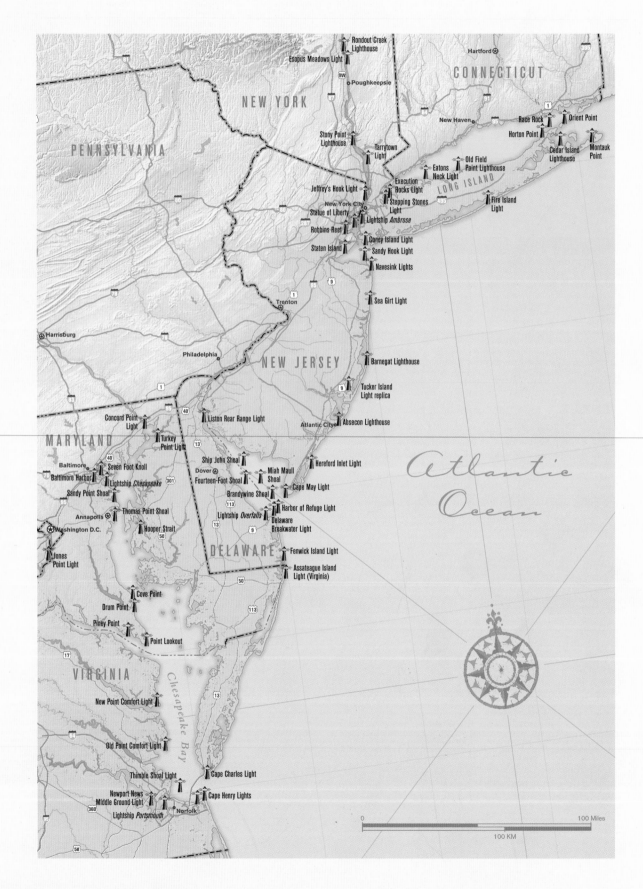

Rondout Creek
Lighthouse

Esopus Meadows Light

Poughkeepsie

Hartford

CONNECTICUT

NEW YORK

PENNSYLVANIA

Stony Point
Lighthouse

Tarrytown
Light

New Haven

Race Rock

Orient Point

Horton Point

Eatons
Neck Light

Old Field
Point Lighthouse

Cedar Island
Lighthouse

Montauk
Point

Jeffrey's Hook Light

Execution
Rocks Light

LONG ISLAND

Stepping Stones
Light

Fire Island
Light

New York City
Statue of Liberty

Lightship Ambrose

Robbins Reef

Coney Island Light

Staten Island

Sandy Hook Light

Navesink Lights

Trenton

Sea Girt Light

Harrisburg

Philadelphia

NEW JERSEY

Barnegat Lighthouse

Tucker Island
Light replica

Concord Point
Light

Liston Rear Range Light

Atlantic City

Absecon Lighthouse

MARYLAND

Turkey
Point Light

Baltimore

Seven Foot Knoll

Ship John Shoal

Hereford Inlet Light

Baltimore Harbor

Dover

Miah Maull
Shoal

Lightship Chesapeake

Fourteen-Foot Shoal

Sandy Point Shoal

Cape May Light

Brandywine Shoal

Annapolis

Thomas Point Shoal

Lightship Overfalls

Harbor of Refuge Light

Washington D.C.

Hooper Strait

Delaware
Breakwater Light

Jones
Point Light

DELAWARE

Fenwick Island Light

Assateague Island
Light (Virginia)

Atlantic
Ocean

Cove Point

Drum Point

Piney Point

Point Lookout

VIRGINIA

Chesapeake Bay

New Point Comfort Light

Old Point Comfort Light

Thimble Shoal Light

Cape Charles Light

Newport News
Middle Ground Light

Cape Henry Lights

Lightship Portsmouth

Norfolk

0   100 Miles

100 KM

CONTENTS

ACKNOWLEDGMENTS

We gratefully acknowledge the assistance of the following people in the making of this book: U.S. Coast Guard Historian Dr. Robert Browning; photographers Bill Kaufhold, Mark Riddick, Bob and Sandra Shanklin, H. Kent Edwards, and Shirin Pagels; Tom Laverty of the Navesink Lighthouse in New Jersey; Candace Clifford of the Maritime Initiative in Washington, D.C.; Jack Barbara of Edison for his assistance with locations of lighthouses in New Jersey; Zoe Madans of New Jersey for generous contacts concerning mid-Atlantic lighthouses; the Mariners Museum Library of Newport News, the Chesapeake Bay Maritime Museum at Saint Michaels, Maryland; and the Calvert Marine Museum in Solomons, Maryland, all of which have excellent historical materials that they made available to us. Finally, our sincerest thanks to Tim Harrison and other members of the American Lighthouse Foundation for their assistance with this book and their continuing support for lighthouses and lighthouse preservation.

Jones Point Lighthouse, Virginia, by the light of the moon
(© Mark Riddick/New Light Photography)

INTRODUCTION

THE ANCIENT GREEKS WERE A SEAFARING PEOPLE, so it should come as no surprise that they included a lighthouse among their Seven Wonders of the World. Along with the Pyramids of Egypt, the Hanging Gardens of Babylon, the Colossus of Rhodes, and the other wonders, they ranked Pharos, history's first great lighthouse, among the most important and spectacular man-made structures of any age. Rising 450 feet into the blue Mediterranean skies, Pharos was also the tallest lighthouse of all time—and, as twelve centuries of nearly continuous operation would prove, the light with the longest service record.

Built about 280 B.C. on an island in the bustling harbor of the Greco-Egyptian city Alexandria, Pharos guided ships to the world's busiest seaport. The light, produced by a fire blazing on the tower's roof, could be seen from nearly 30 miles at sea. Ancient mariners needed the Pharos light because Alexandria stood on the flat Nile Delta, and there were no mountains or other natural features to help them locate the city from the sea.

Peoples had long made a practice of banking fires on hills and mountainsides to bring their sailors home from the sea. With Pharos, its artificial mountain, Alexandria pulled in seamen from the entire known world. The sight of the Pharos light burning far up near the dome of the sky must have filled the breasts of countless sea captains with awe. In time the delta city became the busiest and most prosperous port on Earth, and it remained so for nearly a thousand years.

Trading ships from Greece, Carthage, and Rome flocked to the city's wharves to load up with the grain grown in wondrous abundance along the banks of the Nile. It was for possession of Alexandria and her grain markets that Octavius fought and defeated Antony and Cleopatra. Without Egypt's grain to feed the empire's teeming city masses, Rome's conquests would have been meaningless. And without Pharos, the lumbering Roman grain ships might never have found Alexandria. Thus, in a very real sense, the Roman Empire depended on a lighthouse.

Like Rome, the United States of America is a highly commercial nation, part industrial and part agrarian. As with Rome, the growth and prosperity of the United States has depended on safe navigation of waters leading to its busy port cities. As a result, lighthouses have been a major concern for Americans right from the nation's beginning. This book tells the story of the lighthouses that serve America's vital Mid-Atlantic coast from New York to Virginia.

AMERICA'S OWN TINY PHAROS

America also has a proud old city named Alexandria, and it, too, is a port. Like the first Alexandria, the city in Virginia was once the heart of a rich agricultural region. Today it is a wealthy suburb, located down the Potomac River from the nation's capital.

Alexandria is a historic city. It was here that George Washington, who lived only a short carriage ride away in Mount Vernon, did most of his shopping and socializing. At his club in Alexandria, Washington met with friends and advisers to plan the strategy that would carry him and the nation through the Revolutionary War.

After the war had established America's independence, Alexandria was among the cities proposed to become the nation's new capital. In fact, Alexandria was included within the original boundaries of the District of Columbia, but eventually its citizens chose to cast their lot with agrarian Virginia. At Alexandria's Jones Point, some 5 or 6 miles down the Potomac from the City of Washington, is a stone marking one of the corners of the old 10-square-mile federal district.

Also at Jones Point stands a small, rectangular building with whitewashed wooden walls, a pitched roof, and a raised porch. Probably no more than 20 feet high, its appearance suggests a nineteenth-century country schoolhouse. Except for the tiny lantern protruding from its roof, one might never guess that it had anything in common with the Pharos tower of ancient Egypt's Alexandria. But it does: It is a lighthouse.

Built in 1855, the Jones Point Lighthouse guided trading ships, tugs, and barges into Alexandria, Washington, and nearby Georgetown for more than seventy years. It can now claim distinction as the nation's oldest standing inland lighthouse. In counterpoint to its gargantuan Egyptian ancestor, it is also among the nation's and the world's smallest lighthouses.

Deactivated in 1926, the venerable little lighthouse was abandoned. Eventually it fell into a sad state of disrepair. It might have been torn down had it not been for the intervention of the Daughters of the American Revolution and other groups concerned with the preservation of historic structures.

The story of the Jones Point Lighthouse has a happy ending. It recently received a much-needed facelift, and today it has a new, active life—in 1995, after nearly seven decades of disuse, its lantern was relit. Pleasure craft and other vessels headed up the Potomac at night will now see a light burning on Jones Point, just as Roman sea captains once saw a fire burning over the Nile Delta.

THE LIGHTHOUSE REVOLUTION

Lighthouses were among the flash points where trading ships and history collided to produce the nation we know today. In 1718 Alexander Spotswood, the governor of colonial Virginia, approached the British Board of Trade with a remarkable idea. Why not build a tower on Cape Henry, at the mouth of the Chesapeake, and place a light atop it to guide ships into the bay? Just such a tower had been built a couple of years earlier in Massachusetts, and as a result, Boston Harbor had become a magnet for sea trade almost overnight. Governor Spotswood was certain that a similar structure erected on one of the Virginia capes not only would make the Chesapeake Bay safer for shipping but also would greatly increase commerce in the region. Spotswood told the British that the benefits of the project seemed to him "so obvious that I have often wondered why so useful a work has not been undertaken long ere now."

The Board of Trade listened politely to the governor's proposal and then proceeded to ignore it. The British government had begun to grow suspicious and, perhaps, a touch envious of the swelling prosperity of its colonies in America. Parliament had no intention of spending good British sterling on a project likely to help the business-minded American colonists make still more money. So the British built no lighthouse on Cape Henry. More than half a century later, General Charles Cornwallis may have wished they had.

By the mid-1770s British subjects in the American colonies were fed up with their mother country. They hated paying taxes—even a penny a pound tax on tea—and the negligent attitude of British officials toward needed public projects, such as the building of lighthouses, made the colonists even more obstinate about opening their purses for the king. It seemed to them that His Majesty George III considered them a lot of country bumpkins. Feeling that they were being treated like second-class citizens, increasing numbers of Americans were reaching the conclusion that they must take their destinies into their own hands.

Execution Rocks Light stands guard over a stony shoal, which takes its name from a grim Revolutionary War rumor—that British troops were executing prisoners by chaining them to the rocks and waiting for high tide. First lit in 1850, the station's beacon still guides mariners. (Bob and Sandra Shanklin)

Caught up in the independent spirit sweeping the colonies, the people of Maryland and Virginia decided to pool their resources and build their own lighthouse on Cape Henry. In their view, if the project were left entirely to the British, the mouth of the Chesapeake would be dark forever. But work on the lighthouse had barely started when the alienation of Americans boiled over into open rebellion, and the effort had to be abandoned. Instead of constructing a lighthouse, the colonists now undertook to build a nation of their own.

The Revolutionary War was very hard on lighthouses. The British blew up North America's oldest lighthouse when they retreated from Boston in 1776. Another early light, the Cape Henlopen Lighthouse, which dated to 1765, was snuffed out by the British in 1777. It would not be repaired and back on active duty again until well after the end of the war.

Although the Treaty of Paris, granting Americans their independence from Britain, was not signed until 1783, most historians agree that the war ended in 1781 at Yorktown, Virginia. By August of that year, when General Cornwallis marched his redcoat army into Yorktown, the British had been fighting for five long and wearying years to put down the American revolt.

Tired of the struggle, they had sent Cornwallis to America with orders to bring the war to a speedy conclusion. Tough and ruthless, Cornwallis had no scruples at all about burning people's homes and crops and driving off their livestock. He was sent to America to heap misery on the king's unruly subjects, and, in a series of destructive sweeps through the Carolinas and Virginia during the spring and summer of 1781, that is exactly what he did. Then, believing smugly that he had brought the revolutionaries to their knees, Cornwallis fell back to rest and resupply his troops at Yorktown, a small port located conveniently on the banks of the York River near the point where it flows into the Chesapeake.

Old Cape Henry Lighthouse

Cornwallis had one important flaw as a commander: an arrogant disregard for the military skill of his opponents. He had little respect for the fighting abilities of the French, who had entered the war on the side of the Americans, and even less for George Washington and his rag-tag Continental Army. So, even with his back to the York River and the Chesapeake beyond, Cornwallis felt perfectly safe at Yorktown. Indeed, he was so confident that he neglected to hurry his soldiers in their task of fortifying his new base of operations.

It must have astounded the British general to learn, as he did in mid-September, that Washington's army was closing in on Yorktown. Marching alongside the Virginia planter and his soldiers was a large body of French infantry as well as a second army under the Marquis de Lafayette. The startled Cornwallis realized that he would soon be dangerously outnumbered.

But the general remained calm. He knew that he had a resource near at hand that the Americans could not hope to match—the British Navy. He had every reason to believe that a fleet of friendly ships would soon appear and, with their massed cannons, send his enemies fleeing into the woods. Cornwallis felt sure that, at the very least, he could count on the Royal Navy to evacuate his troops.

Exactly as Cornwallis thought, help was on its way; a large British squadron of twenty-seven ships, commanded by Admiral Thomas Graves, was pushing south from New York under full sail. But the relief squadron never reached Yorktown. Just as Graves cut eastward toward the Chesapeake at the Virginia capes, he slammed into an unexpected obstacle: A powerful fleet of thirty-six French warships under Rear Admiral De Grasse blocked the way. Had there been a light on Cape Henry to show the way, Graves might have slipped past the French fleet in the night, entered the Chesapeake, and rescued the beleaguered Cornwallis. But with no light on the cape to guide his ships, Graves dared not attempt such a maneuver. He had no alternative but to attack. Cannons flashed and thundered for hour after hour. When the battle was over, three British fighting ships had been sunk and the rest were fleeing north in disorder.

Cornwallis's proud redcoats now found themselves tightly squeezed between Americans and French to their front and the York River at their back. The British crouched low in their trenches as cannonballs rained in from several directions. The artillery barrage became so fierce that Cornwallis had to move his headquarters into a cave under the bluffs along the Yorktown water-front. To prevent French ships from sailing into the harbor and shelling him from the rear, Cornwallis created artificial shoals in the river by scuttling supply boats.

The British fought on for several weeks, but with no help coming from beyond the capes, the outcome of the siege was no longer in question. On October 20, 1781, their band playing a tune called "The World Turned Upside Down," the redcoats marched out from behind their fortifications and surrendered. The Americans had won the Revolutionary War and with it the right to collect their own taxes—and, if they wished, to build their own lighthouses.

What course might history have taken if the British had built a lighthouse on the Virginia Capes shortly after 1718, when the colonists first asked for it? Had the British been more solicitous of the colonists and paid closer attention to their needs, maybe there would never have been a revolution in the first place. Even if the split was inevitable, the Battle of Yorktown and the war itself might have turned out differently if there had been a lighthouse on Cape Henry to guide the British fleet to Cornwallis's rescue.

Roughly a dozen years after the Yorktown siege and less than ten years after the Treaty of Paris made the American independence official, the U.S. government built a lighthouse on Cape Henry. Completed in 1792, it stood very near the place where, a lifetime earlier, Spotswood had envisioned a tower. Spotswood died in 1740, many years before the Revolution, independence, and construction of the Cape Henry Lighthouse. But, had he lived to see it, the sight of a light burning on the cape would surely have brought a knowing smile to his face.

Eatons Neck Light (William Kaufhold)

CHAPTER ONE

LIGHTS AT THE GOLDEN DOOR
New York

A FARMER AND A LIFELONG LANDLUBBER, George Washington rarely went to sea, but, like Governor Spotswood before him, he was a friend and enthusiastic promoter of lighthouses. In 1789, as president, Washington urged the very first U.S. Congress to pass legislation taking federal control of all coastal lighthouses. At that time the nation had only a few scattered lights to mark more than 2,000 miles of coast.

Staten Island Light (William Kaufhold)

AMERICAN LIGHTHOUSES IN 1789

Built on Little Brewster Island near the outer edge of Boston Harbor, Boston Light (1716) was North America's first lighthouse. A cylindrical stone structure with a lantern room at the top, it set the pattern for many of the hundreds of lighthouses that would be built afterward. Destroyed in Revolutionary War raids by both Continental and British forces, it was rebuilt in 1783.

Marking the entrance to Nantucket Harbor, in Massachusetts, Brant Point Light (1746) was the second lighthouse built in the original thirteen colonies. A rather flimsy wooden structure, it burned or was blown over in storms several times only to be rebuilt by the island's tenacious whalers and fishermen, who depended on it for guidance. The Brant Point Lighthouse had burned to the ground in 1786 and had not yet been replaced at the time that Washington became president.

America's third lighthouse, Beavertail Light (1749), marked the passage into Rhode Island's Narragansett Bay. Its square, rubblestone tower anchored the southern tip of sandy Conanicut Island, which the pirate captain William Kidd had used as a hideout during the 1600s. Like the Boston Light, this one was knocked out of operation by the British during the Revolutionary War. By 1790, however, it was repaired and back in service.

Built with the proceeds of a public lottery, New London Light (1760) survived the Revolutionary War intact. Continental privateers often used the light to help find refuge from pursuing British warships.

An octagonal brick structure, Sandy Hook Light (1764) stood near the mouth of the Hudson River and showed the way to New York City's bustling harbor. New Yorkers had financed and built this strategic light tower, but, since it was actually located in New Jersey, the legislature of the Garden State laid claim to the facility following the Revolutionary War. This precipitated a protracted and often heated legal squabble between the two states. The matter was settled only when Congress took control of this and other U.S. lighthouses in 1789 (see pages 38–39).

Guiding ships into Delaware Bay and the river beyond, Cape Henlopen Light (1765) was one of the most important navigational markers in America. For sea captains caught in a storm, the light was a particularly welcome sight, as it marked one of the few safe harbors along the entire Eastern Seaboard. Even in the worst weather, the waters behind the cape were nearly always calm. Burned by British sailors and marines in 1777, Cape Henlopen Lighthouse was repaired and relit in 1784 (see pages 55–57).

Charleston Light (1767), located on sandy Morris Island, which was frequently inundated by high tides, pointed the way to the harbor of one of North America's oldest and most gracious cities. For decades it was the only significant navigational light south of the Virginia capes.

Serving the famed Massachusetts community founded by the Pilgrims, Plymouth Light (1768) was unique in that it displayed not one but two lights from the same building. The twin beacons set the light apart from ordinary lanterns marking nearby harbors.

During its early years Portsmouth Light (1771) consisted of little more than a lantern hoisted up the flagpole of Fort William and Mary, on the banks of New Hampshire's Piscataqua River. In 1775 the keeper felt free temporarily to set aside his duties and take a wagonload of gunpowder to the embattled Massachusetts Minutemen on Bunker Hill. A proper wood-frame lighthouse was eventually built here. During the 1780s it received a pair of famous visitors: the Revolutionary War hero General Marquis de Lafayette and his old commander, George Washington himself.

Built to warn mariners away from Thacher Island, a barren, ship-killing rock off the north coast of Massachusetts, Cape Ann Lighthouse (1771) consisted of two separate towers. The island was named for a colonial clergyman and his family shipwrecked here in 1635. The station's first keeper was a notorious Tory. When the Revolutionary War broke out, a party of Massachusetts militiamen hustled him off the island, plunging the twin lights into darkness until after the war.

The second lighthouse to be established on tiny Nantucket, Great Point Light (1784) stood at the northern end of the island. Although it was built of wood like the neighboring Brant Point Lighthouse, it proved more durable. It had stood for five years by the time the federal government took control of the nation's lighthouses.

Intended to guide ships safely over the treacherous sandbar at the harbor entrance, Newburyport Light (1788) was the first known use of a range-light system. Two lights were displayed, one higher and some distance behind the other. The lights appeared in perpendicular alignment only to ships in safe water.

THE UNITED STATES LIGHTHOUSE SERVICE

Anxious to encourage commerce, President Washington recognized that the new nation's system of coastal lights was woefully inadequate. Under pressure from the president, Congress made lighthouses a priority and, in one of its very first official acts, created the United States Lighthouse Service. In one form or another, the service would survive for more than 150 years, right up until the U.S. Coast Guard took full responsibility for the nation's navigational aids in 1939. By that time nearly 1,000 fine lighthouses marked the Atlantic and Gulf coasts in the East, the Pacific and Bering Sea coasts in the West, and the shores of the Great Lakes in the Midwest.

A century and a half earlier, however, when the Lighthouse Service was in its infancy, the number of operational lights was pitifully small, including only the eleven functional lights described above (the Brant Point Lighthouse was out of service at that time). To remedy this, the service undertook a major construction program that added a dozen major lights during the 1790s, the nation's first full decade of independence. These were the lighthouses at Cape Henry, Virginia (completed in 1791); Portland Head, Maine (1791); Tybee, Georgia (1791); Seguin, Maine (1795); Bald Head, North Carolina (1796); Montauk Point, New York (1797); Baker's Island, Massachusetts (1798); Cape Cod, Massachusetts (1798); Cape Hatteras, North Carolina (1798); Ocracoke, North Carolina (1798); Gay Head, Massachusetts (1799); and Eatons Neck, New York (1799).

Perhaps appropriately, this initial burst of lighthouse construction was completed shortly before George Washington died during the final weeks of 1799. The old general missed by only seventeen days witnessing the beginning of the nineteenth century and, with it, the opening of a whole new era of expansion and prosperity. As a revolutionary, signer of the Declaration of Independence, leader of the Continental Army, framer of the Constitution, and the nation's first president, Washington had done more than almost any American to make this new and optimistic age possible. Among his most important contributions, however, was one that is not frequently recognized: his insistence on an efficient system of lights for America's coasts and navigable inland waters.

THE LIBERTY LIGHTS

Lighthouses make navigation easier and safer, but they also serve as symbols, both profound and practical, welcoming sailors from other lands to our shores. For many of the millions of immigrants who came to America in search of opportunity and a better life, the first glimpse of their new home was the beacon of a distant lighthouse. Likely, the light most often seen first by approaching immigrants was that of the Montauk Point Lighthouse, built in 1797 at the far end of Long Island. For others it may have been the Boston Lighthouse, the Cape Hatteras Lighthouse on North Carolina's Outer Banks, the Cape Henry or Cape Charles Lighthouses at the entrance of the Chesapeake Bay, or any one of dozens of other prominent coastal lights.

Montauk Point Light, Long Island

America's most widely known symbol of freedom is, of course, the Statue of Liberty. Striking a bold pose on the island near the entrance to the New York City Harbor, the statue has welcomed visitors and immigrants to America for more than a century. With its bright lantern thrusting more than 300 feet above the water, the statue was intended to serve as a lighthouse. For many years it was recognized as an official harbor light, useful to vessels moving up and down the Hudson River or headed for the city wharves.

Known officially as the "Statue of Liberty Enlightening the World," it was the dream of a nineteenth-century French historian named Edouard de Laboulaye, a passionate admirer of American political institutions. Laboulaye raised money for the project in France, hired Frederic Auguste Bartholdi to design the statue, and, when it was completed in 1884, presented it to the United States as a gesture of French–American friendship. The dismantled statue arrived in New York in 214 enormous packing crates. Reassembled on twelve-acre Bedloe Island, now known as Liberty Island, it was dedicated in 1886 by President Grover Cleveland.

The statue appears today almost exactly as it did more than a century ago, but it has required continual maintenance and care. During its centennial in 1986, it received a multimillion-dollar renovation, which included replacement of the 1,600 wrought-iron bands that hold the copper skin to its iron frame.

The statue weighs approximately 450,000 pounds. From her heel to the top of her head, the lady stands 111 feet tall. Her toenails are more than a foot across.

Her most heroic quality, however, is not her extraordinary size but, rather, the very powerful idea she represents. A symbol recognized the world over, she is freedom's lighthouse. Perhaps the Emma Lazarus poem engraved on a tablet at the statue's base conveys this message best. It reads:

> *Not like the brazen giant of Greek fame,*
> *With conquering limbs astride from land to land;*
> *Here at our sea-washed, sunset gates shall stand*
> *A mighty woman with a torch, whose flame*
> *Is the imprisoned lightning, and her name*
> *Mother of Exiles. From her beacon-hand*
> *Glows world-wide welcome; her mild eyes command*
> *The air-bridged harbor that twin cities frame.*
> *"Keep ancient lands, your storied pomp!" cries she*
> *With silent lips. "Give me your tired, your poor,*
> *Your huddled masses yearning to breathe free,*
> *The wretched refuse of your teeming shore.*
> *Send these, the homeless, tempest-tost to me,*
> *I lift my lamp beside the golden door!"*

Statue of Liberty (William Kaufhold)

MONTAUK POINT LIGHT

Long Island, New York — 1797

The prominent bluff at the far eastern extremity of Long Island reminded early European settlers of the hump in a turtle's back, so they called the place Turtle Hill. But the unpretentious name belies the importance of this strategic point of land.

Long before the arrival of the white man, the first beacons burned on the hill known to Indians as Womponamon. According to legend, leaders of the powerful Montauk tribe lit signal fires at the summit of the hill to call their chiefs and warriors to council. The vessels guided by this light were dugout canoes carved from the trunks of large trees.

Some say that the British also banked bright fires on the hill. During the Revolutionary War several of King George's ships lay off Montauk Point in order to blockade Long Island Sound. The fires served these warships as beacons.

After the war the new U.S. government recognized that it must follow the example of the British and the Indians before them. Such a significant and dangerous headland could not be left unmarked, and President George Washington himself ordered construction of a lighthouse on Montauk Point. It was to be an expensive project. Contractor John McComb of New York

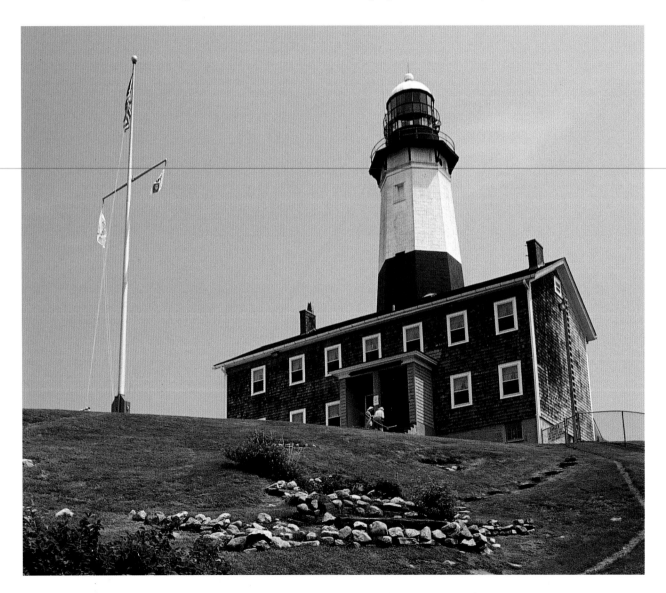

submitted a low bid of $22,300 to dig foundations, haul sandstone, and build the tower and two-story keeper's dwelling. At a time when lighthouses elsewhere were being built for as little as $2,000, this was a hefty price. Land for the light station had been purchased for only a little more than $250. But McComb gave the country its money's worth. He built the lighthouse like a fortress, with a foundation 13 feet deep and walls 7 feet thick at the base. As a consequence, the Montauk Point Lighthouse still stands after more than two centuries of blasting by Atlantic storms. McComb was also the contractor for a lighthouse erected in 1791 on Cape Henry in Virginia. The tower he built there, though unused for more than a century, stands to this day.

Generations of immigrants caught their first sight of America at Montauk Point, and the lighthouse there became for many of them a symbol of the freedom and opportunity waiting for them in their new country. That the old light tower should fall is unthinkable; it would be as jarring as if someone chiseled the faces off the side of Mount Rushmore or bowled over the Statue of Liberty.

The Montauk Point Light continues to guide ships more than two centuries after its lamps first burned. Not all the sailors who have seen the light, however, have reached port safely. Storms have driven many vessels against the beaches near Montauk, usually with disastrous results. Some ships got permanently stuck in the sand, others broke in half and sank, and a few "melted like a lump of sugar" in the raging surf. More than a century ago, local residents told a correspondent for *Harper's New Monthly* magazine about "how a ship was driven ashore one wild night . . . how brave men gathered to the rescue; how the crew, one after another dropped into the sea, some of them being saved from the jaws of the angry waves; of a mother washed ashore, dead, clasping a babe in her arms; the wild figures of the wreckers on that dark, stormy night of horrors, lit up by a great fire of drift-wood. . . . "

Ships are not the only wrecks found on the Montauk beaches. Whales occasionally end their days there as well. For reasons that are still not understood, whales sometimes beach themselves on the shores of Long Island (and elsewhere). Unless they can be coaxed or winched back into the ocean, they

Years ago, this double-lamp, airport-style lighting system replaced a first-order Fresnel lens at Montauk.

die. Long Island settlers and, no doubt, the Indians before them were quite familiar with the phenomenon of beached whales. The first pastor of the church at East Hampton, a few miles from Montauk, received as his salary "forty-five pounds annually, lands rate free, grain to be first ground at the mill every Monday, and one-fourth of the whales stranded on the beach."

For many decades the lamps of the lighthouse at Montauk Point burned whale oil, though it was a commercial variety and was not taken from the unfortunate animals that happened onto nearby beaches. By the mid-1850s whalers had decimated the world's whale population. Seeing that it could no longer count on a regular supply of whale oil, the Lighthouse Service switched to lard oil as a fuel here and elsewhere. Later many lighthouse lamps, including those at Montauk, burned kerosene.

HOW TO GET THERE: *Follow Route 27 to Montauk Point State Park, at the far eastern end of Long Island. If you could visit only one lighthouse in America, the Montauk Light would be a good choice. The museum in the old keeper's dwelling displays an outstanding collection of nautical and lighthouse artifacts, including several classic Fresnel lenses. The museum is well worth the small admission charge, which goes toward preservation of the lighthouse. For more information call (631) 668–2544.*

ORIENT POINT LIGHT

Orient Point, New York — 1899

ust off the northeastern tip of Long Island, a deep but narrow passage called Plum Gut links several heavily trafficked bodies of water, including Long Island Sound and Gardiners Bay. Strong currents make navigating any part of the Gut a tricky business. But a helmsman's chief concern is Oyster Pond Reef, a deadly ledge lurking just beneath the surface of the water and extending fully one-third of the way across the waterway.

To mark this unseen menace, in 1896 the Lighthouse Board approved construction of a caisson-type tower in the open water at the far end of the reef. The Orient Point Lighthouse took two years to build and was not operational until 1899. It cost $30,000, about six times the original estimate for the project. To protect the structure from high waves driven by gales, the builders piled hundreds of tons of broken stone around its base. Painted brown at the top and white at the bottom, the cast-iron tower was not particularly handsome. It was soon given the nickname

"Coffee Pot" by mariners who passed regularly through Plum Gut.

The station's first keeper was N. A. Anderson, a Norwegian immigrant. He was married, but because his isolated light station was considered too small and dangerous for a woman, his wife lived in the town of Orient on Long Island. Anderson served for twenty years in the Coffee Pot at a salary of $50 a month.

Now unmanned and automated, the Orient Point Light guides maritime traffic with a white flash every five seconds. The tower stands 64 feet above the water, and its light can be seen for 15 miles.

HOW TO GET THERE: *The lighthouse cannot be reached by land but can be seen from Orient Point, New York. It can also be seen from the ferry connecting New London, Connecticut, and Orient Point. For ferry schedules, fares, and other information, call (860) 443–5281.*

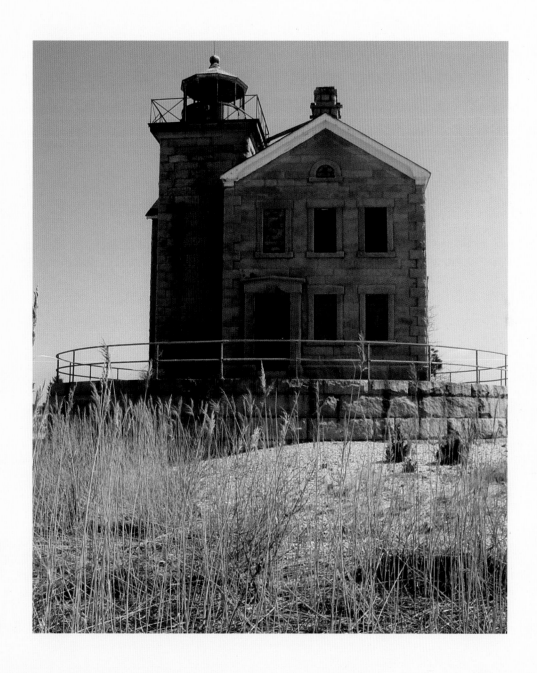

Built in 1868, the **Cedar Island Lighthouse** *served the old whaling community of Sag Harbor, near the eastern tip of Long Island. The two-story granite dwelling and 40-foot tower replaced an earlier lighthouse in operation here since 1839. The station was abandoned in 1934, when a nearby skeleton tower was completed. Local historical organizations hope to restore the original structure to its former glory. (Shirin Pagels)*

RACE ROCK LIGHT

Race Rock, near Fishers Island, New York — 1879

Although it is positioned only about 5 miles from Watch Hill, Rhode Island, and less than 8 miles from New London, Connecticut, the Race Rock Lighthouse is actually located in the state of New York. It stands on a high stone pier near where three state boundaries come together just off the tip of New York's Fishers Island.

Built at great expense and through almost superhuman effort during the late 1870s, the lighthouse marks an extraordinarily dangerous shoal known as Race Point Reef. Strong currents rushing back and forth between Long Island Sound and the Atlantic make this area a nightmare for sailors. Mariners long ago gave it the nickname the "horse race."

Built in open water atop a massive concrete pier, the Race Rock Lighthouse took eight years and several substantial federal appropriations to complete. It warns ships away from a deadly shoal near the entrance to Long Island Sound. (Bob and Sandra Shanklin)

A long list of ships have come to grief on Fishers Island and the nearby coasts of Connecticut and Rhode Island, but Race Point Reef itself is particularly vicious. During the 1700s and early 1800s, the reef sank ships at a rate of nearly one per year. In 1829 alone the reef claimed at least eight ships, and there likely were other wrecks that went unreported. Mariners described the reef as a "killer."

In 1838 Congress appropriated $3,000 to build a lighthouse on Race Rock, but this sum was so pitifully inadequate that construction was put on hold indefinitely. Meanwhile the carnage continued. Perhaps the worst disaster occurred in 1846, when the passenger steamer *Atlantic* slammed into Race Point Reef, with a loss of fifty-seven lives. Despite this calamity, it was not until 1869 that Congress finally appropriated a more realistic sum, $90,000, to build the lighthouse.

But even this—at the time quite substantial funding—would prove insufficient. Before the Race Rock light station was complete, its price tag would balloon to $278,716, placing it, comparatively speaking, among the most expensive lighthouses ever built. It was also one of the most remarkable engineering feats of its era.

Construction of a lighthouse in the open waters of Long Island Sound proved a daunting task. To attempt it federal officials employed F. Hopkinson Smith, a well-known construction engineer, to bring the project to fruition. Smith in turn hired as his foreman Thomas Scott, a sharp-tongued former ship's captain whom he described as a "bifurcated sea dog." The work began in 1871, and before it was completed more than eight years later, Scott would employ every foul phrase he had learned as a sailor and, no doubt, would invent some more.

First a pier had to be constructed in 13 feet of often turbulent water. To this purpose, Smith and Scott tried building an artificial island by dumping tons of stone onto Race Rock. Enormous loads of broken rocks and boulders—10,000 tons in all—were poured onto the site, but the strong currents swept away the fill almost as fast as boats could deliver it. Frustrated, Smith and Scott resorted to the much slower and more expensive method of having divers lay cement on the sea bottom. This process took nearly two years but eventually produced a mass of concrete some 9 feet thick and 69 feet in diameter. Upon this pad they were able to construct a stone pier.

The job was still far from finished. Progress was impeded by storms, ice, sunken supply barges, exhausted funding, appropriation delays, and the death of two workmen in separate accidents. In all, it took almost a decade to complete the pier and lighthouse. It was not until February 21, 1879, that a keeper climbed the steps of the tower and lit the lamps for the first time. Nonetheless, mariners fighting the five-knot currents of the "horse race" were glad enough to see it.

Built of large granite blocks, the two-story Race Rock Lighthouse stands on a massive stone pier rising almost 30 feet above high water. The attached square tower places the light approximately 67 feet above the surface of Long Island Sound. The automated light alternates between red and white flashes and can be seen from 14 miles away.

HOW TO GET THERE: *While the Race Rock Lighthouse can be reached only by water, its light can be seen from Watch Hill, Rhode Island, and several points along the Connecticut coast. The ferries from New London, Connecticut, to Orient Point, New York, and Block Island, Rhode Island, often pass within sight of Race Rock. The ferries operate only during the summer. For prices and schedules call (401) 783–4613. Incidentally, New London, Watch Hill, and Block Island have delightful lighthouses of their own, all worth a visit (see* New England Lighthouses, *second edition, The Globe Pequot Press, 2005).*

HORTON POINT LIGHT

Southold, New York — 1790 AND 1857

n 1757, during the French and Indian War, a young military officer from Virginia paused atop one of the high bluffs of Southold, New York, and gazed thoughtfully down onto Long Island Sound. He had come here to see firsthand a notorious stretch of coast known to locals and to the survivors of no few shipwrecks as "Dead Man's Cove." The Virginian told his companions that someday a lighthouse would be built on the very spot where he was standing. His name was George Washington, and many years later, in 1790, while serving as the nation's first president, he would commission the lighthouse himself.

In June 1990 the Horton Point Lighthouse celebrated the 200th anniversary of its commissioning. The event, attended by dignitaries and many friends of the old lighthouse, was doubly significant. On that same day the light was restored to active service after standing dark for fifty-eight years, the Coast Guard having decommissioned the lighthouse in 1933.

The Horton Point Lighthouse seen today was built on the bluffs during the mid-1850s. In June 1857, a century after Washington first visited the place, the whale-oil lamps were lit and the third-order Fresnel lamp began to throw light out over the Sound.

From 1903 to 1904 Stella Prince served as keeper of the Horton Point Lighthouse. Born and raised in the lighthouse itself, she was the daughter of an earlier keeper. Appointed by President Theodore Roosevelt, she was one of only a few women ever to receive an official appointment as a lighthouse keeper.

HOW TO GET THERE: *From Route 25 or Route 48 in Southold, follow Horton Lane toward Long Island Sound. Turn right onto Sound View Road and then left onto Lighthouse Road. The Southold Historical Society operates a delightful nautical museum at the lighthouse. For hours and additional information, call (631) 765–5500.*

The **Old Field Point Lighthouse**, near Stony Brook, New York, marks one of several fingers of land that push forward from Long Island and menace shipping in Long Island Sound. Built of granite in 1823, the tower is 35 feet high. Its fourth-order Fresnel lens was recently replaced by an airport-style beacon. The grounds are open to the public and can be reached via Old Field Road off Main Street in Stony Brook. Passengers on the Bridgeport–Port Jefferson ferry get an excellent view of this fine old lighthouse. For schedules or reservations call (631) 473–0286. (Bob and Sandra Shanklin)

EATONS NECK LIGHT

Asharoken, New York — 1799

One of only a handful of surviving eighteenth-century light towers, the Eatons Neck Light near Asharoken on Long Island remains in operation today after nearly 200 years of service. Established to guide ships into Huntington Bay and through the western reaches of Long Island Sound, it was com-pleted in 1799, during the administration of John Adams, the nation's second president.

Like many early lighthouses, this one was built with fieldstone, most of it gathered locally. Even so, time has proven the work remarkably sound. To supervise construction of the tower and dwelling, the

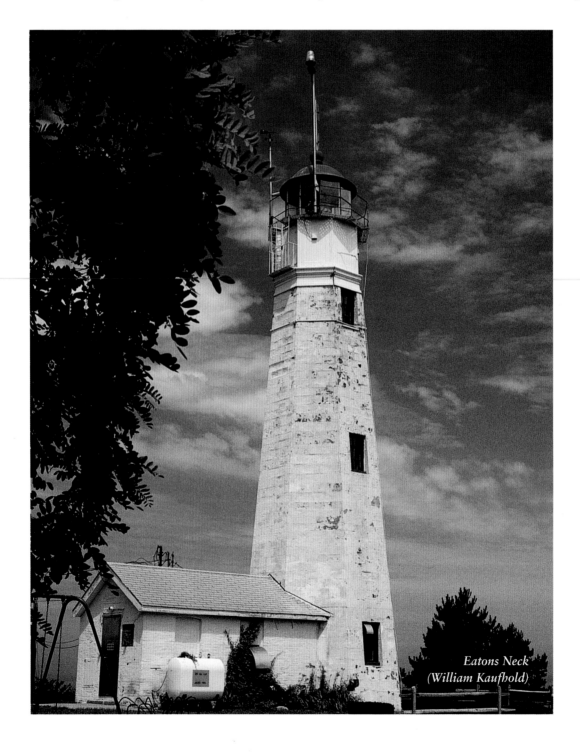

*Eatons Neck
(William Kaufhold)*

government hired John McComb, who also served as contractor for the Montauk Point and Cape Henry Lighthouses. Obviously, McComb built structures intended to last, as these two towers and the 70-foot octagonal tower at Eatons Neck still stand after two centuries of storm, rain, and wind. The Eatons Neck Lighthouse received substantial repairs and renovation in 1868. Otherwise, it has required only minor patching and fixing and remains today essentially the same structure that McComb built in 1799.

Originally equipped with only a simple oil lamp, the lantern displayed a weak light visible from just a few miles out into the sound. Eventually, the station was fitted with an Argand lamp and reflector system designed by Winslow Lewis. The highly polished, 13-inch reflectors provided a more powerful light, but the Lewis system was decidedly inferior to the Fresnel lenses manufactured by the French. For many years Fifth Auditor Stephen Pleasonton of the Treasury Department resisted adoption of the Fresnel system because of the high cost of the hand-polished glass lenses—and, some would say, because of his preference for Lewis. (By the time Eatons Neck Light received its third-order Fresnel in 1856, Pleasonton was no longer head of the U.S. Lighthouse Service.)

Since this area is frequently blanketed by fog, early Eatons Neck keepers spent many hours striking the station's bell. During the 1868 renovation the bell was replaced by a siren. In 1904 an automated foghorn took over the task of warning fog-blinded mariners.

Although the station is still used as a dwelling by Coast Guard personnel, the light itself is automated. Since the tower stands on a bank nearly equal to its own height, the light shines from a lofty 140 feet above the waters of the sound. Well to the west of Eatons Neck, the Stepping Stones Light at Kings Point and Execution Rocks Light near New Rochelle help mark the far western end of Long Island Sound. The 60-foot granite tower and attached two-story keeper's dwelling of the Execution Rocks Lighthouse were built in 1850 (see page 3), while the Stepping Stones Lighthouse dates to 1877. Accessible only by boat, these historic structures can be seen from a number of points along the shore.

HOW TO GET THERE: *On Long Island follow Route 26A through Cold Spring Harbor and Centerport, then turn left at the sign for Asharoken and Eatons Neck. The lighthouse is located at the very end of Lighthouse Road. The tower is located on an active Coast Guard station and is not usually open to the public. To obtain special permission to visit, call (631) 261–6959.*

A neighbor of Eatons Neck, not far from Kings Point, New York, Stepping Stones Light was established in 1877. The distinctive square brick tower and attached residence were once occupied by full-time keepers. The dwelling has been boarded up for years, but the station's automated beacon remains active. (Bob and Sandra Shanklin)

FIRE ISLAND LIGHT

Fire Island, New York — 1826 AND 1858

n 1850 the SS *Elizabeth* struck the sandy shoals off the south coast of Long Island and sank almost within sight of the Fire Island Light station. Ironically, the ship's captain had been looking for the light when he hit the shoals. Many of the *Elizabeth*'s crew drowned, and the disaster precipitated a public outcry. Mariners complained that the 74-foot Fire Island tower, built in 1826, was far too short to accomplish its task of warning sailors away from the shoals.

Although Congress quickly appropriated money to rebuild the lighthouse and raise the height of the tower, nothing was done until 1857, when construction began at last. By that time the Lighthouse Board had launched a major effort to revamp the nation's sadly deteriorated system of navigational lights. Some lighthouses were repointed and repaired, while others were pulled down and replaced altogether. Lantern rooms all along the Eastern Seaboard received improved lamps and the marvelously effective Fresnel lenses made in Paris.

The plan for Fire Island included a new tower nearly twice as high as the original. When masons laid the last brick on the tower during the fall of 1858, it stood 180 feet above the ground. A steel circular staircase with 192 steps led to the lantern room. The low, sandy island gave the tower a boost of about 17 feet, so the station's new Fresnel lens flashed its message to ships at sea from a point 197 feet above the water.

The Lighthouse Board long considered the Fire Island Light one of its most important light stations. Because of its flashing characteristic, the light is known affectionately to many as "Winking Woman."

Decommissioned by the Coast Guard, Fire Island Light went dark in 1974. But it burns brightly again now, thanks to the efforts of a local preservation society.

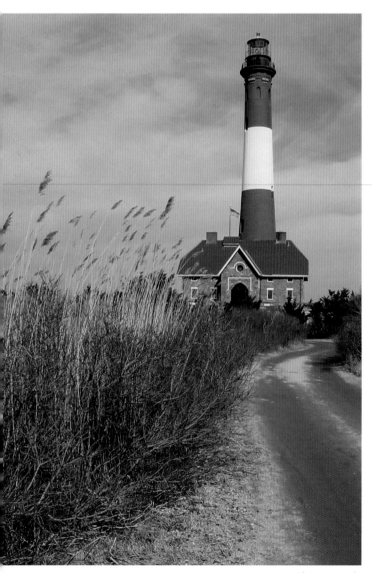

Shirin Pagels

HOW TO GET THERE: *The light can be reached by road from West Islip or by ferry from Bay Shore. The light stands high above the low, sandy barrier island. Once on the island, just head toward the lighthouse; you can't miss it. The Fire Island Preservation Society has restored and relit the old 1858 light, installed an interpretive center in the living quarters, and established a foundation to maintain the station. To contact the society call (516) 321–7028.*

When its temporary beacon first shined late in the year 1826, the **Stony Point Lighthouse** became the government's first operational light on the Hudson River. Its final lighting apparatus, installed in 1902, was a fourth-order Fresnel used previously at the Tarry-town Lighthouse (see page 94). Erected some 20 miles south of West Point, Stony Point's 24-foot structure housed a light that could be seen nearly 22 miles south along the river. Replaced by a skeleton tower in 1925, the original lighthouse now stands high on a promontory in a beautiful state park.

LIGHTHOUSES OF NEW YORK CITY

Robbins Reef — 1883
Statue of Liberty — 1886
Coney Island — 1890
Jeffrey's Hook — 1920

For more than two centuries, New York has been America's most important port, and not surprisingly the city is ringed by maritime lights. Ships approaching the city are guided by a whole series of navigational beacons, but few of them shine from traditional light towers. Some are bridge lights and others simple post lights or lighted buoys placed by the Coast Guard to help vessels keep safely within the proper channel. However, the city is still served by lighthouses.

Although hardly impressive compared to the city's skyscrapers, the **Robbins Reef Lighthouse** is one of New York's most historic buildings. Built in 1883 to mark a dangerous shoal off Staten Island, it has guided countless thousands of passenger ships and freighters to the docks in Manhattan and along the Hudson River. The light has been automated since 1996, but for many years keepers lived and worked full time at this offshore station. The cast-iron, coffeepot-style tower offered little room for family life. Even so, keeper Kate Walker raised several children here and regularly rowed them ashore to go to school on Staten Island. Walker served as keeper from 1886 until 1919, a stretch of thirty-three years, during which she was credited with saving a number of sailors and boaters from drowning.

While some might say that Kate Walker had an iron constitution, another "lady" associated with New York navigational lights was actually made of metal. Dedicated in 1886 and commissioned as a harbor light that same year, the **Statue of Liberty** is probably the world's most famous lighthouse. The light in the bronze lady's torch guided ships in and out of the harbor for many years and is still seen as a guiding light by many landlubbers. Although the lady herself is 151 feet tall, the torch reaches 305 feet above the ground, making this one of America's loftiest navigational lights.

While Lady Liberty is New York's best-known lighthouse, the city has others. For instance, the **Coney Island Light** is assigned the distinctly blue-collar task of guiding the city's garbage barges to the watery dumps in the Atlantic. Established in 1890, the light once guided hulking iron freighters to their Coney Island loading docks. The 68-foot tower consists of a central cylinder crowned by a gallery and lantern

Robbins Reef marks a dangerous shoal obstructing a key channel leading to New York City. (Bob and Sandra Shanklin)

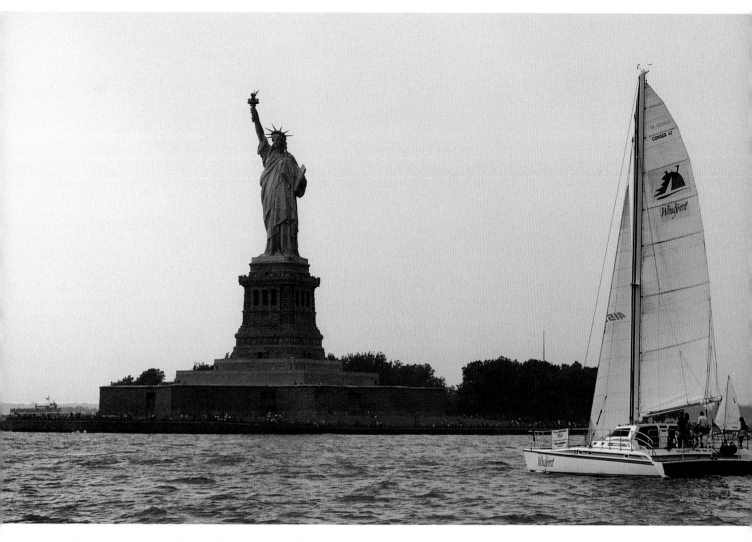

Although few think of it as a lighthouse, the Statue of Liberty once held aloft a harbor beacon guiding vessels in and out of New York. (William Kaufhold)

room and braced by four steel legs. Originally this workmanlike-structure lighthouse displayed the rear member of a pair of range lights. The front range light was taken out of service shortly before the turn of the twentieth century, but the rear range light remains in operation to this day, displaying a flashing red light with a range of more than 15 miles.

Among the city's light towers, the most widely known among children may be the diminutive **Jeffrey's Hook Lighthouse,** celebrated in Hildegarde Hoyt Swift's classic book *The Little Red Lighthouse and the Great Gray Bridge.* There may be no greater architectural contrast than that presented by the tiny red lighthouse that stands beside the mighty George Washington Bridge. Built in 1920, the squat cast-iron

tower took the place of a pair of stake lights, which had stood here since 1889. Only eleven years later, completion of the bridge's massive 3,500-foot central span made the lighthouse obsolete. The Coast Guard intended to auction off the tower as scrap metal and would have done so if not for the public outcry raised in part by publication of Swift's book. It still stands as a sort of monument to the little and forgotten things in this world.

HOW TO GET THERE: *Robbins Reef Lighthouse: This lighthouse is best seen from the water. The Staten Island Ferry provides an excellent view. For more information call (212) 269–5755. The flashing green light of Robbins Reef remains in operation.*

Coney Island Light (William Kaufhold)

Statue of Liberty: The ferry to Liberty Island and the statue leaves from Battery Park at the lower tip of Manhattan. Passengers can also view the Robbins Reef Lighthouse.

Coney Island Lighthouse: From I–278 follow the Prospect Parkway and Ocean Parkway to Coney Island. The lighthouse is on Surf Avenue between 46th and 47th Avenues in the community of Seagate. The fourth-order Fresnel lens that shined in the Coney Island tower until the station was automated in 1989 is on display in the South Street Seaport Museum in 732–7678 or (212) 669–9400.

Jeffrey's Hook Lighthouse: The long-abandoned tower, kept painted bright red by New York City park workers, stands directly under the George Washington Bridge on the Manhattan side of the Hudson. Take the Fort Washington exit off Riverside Drive.

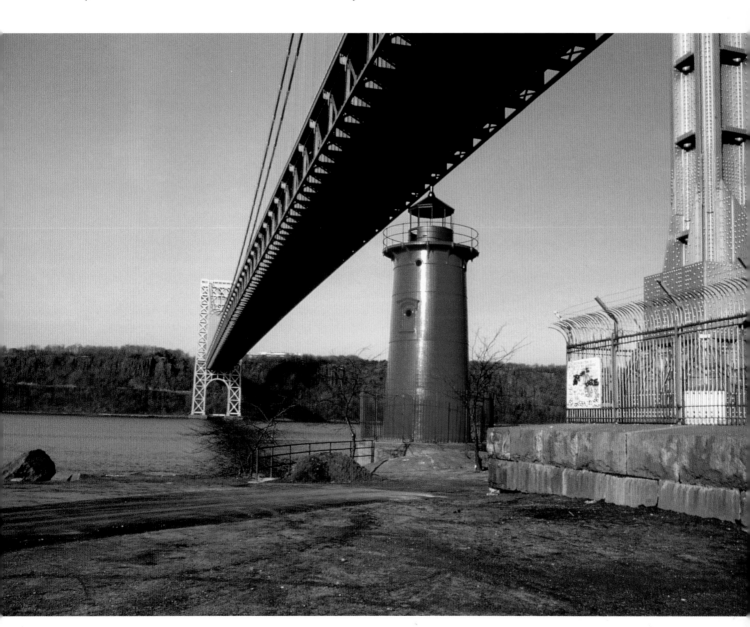

Known to many children as "The Little Red Lighthouse," Jeffrey's Hook tower stands beneath New York's George Washington Bridge.

LIGHTSHIP *AMBROSE*

New York City, New York — 1907

America's once-proud fleet of lightships has been retired, but for many years these little vessels guided ships and marked obstacles in remote areas that even the most powerful lighthouse beacons could not reach. They remained anchored at their duty stations, often for months at a time. Equipment failures, ice floes—even hurricanes could not knock them off their posts for long.

Among the sturdiest of these floating lighthouses was the lightship *Ambrose*. Built in the Camden, New Jersey, shipyards in 1907, it served at one duty station for more than sixty years. Christened with the rather unpoetical name *Lightship No. 87*, its first assignment was in the Ambrose Channel, leading to New York City. On station there for nearly a quarter of a century, it became known to passing sailors and lightship crewmen as the *Ambrose*.

Only 135 feet long and with a beam of 29 feet, the 680-ton *Ambrose* was tiny compared to the huge freighters and passenger liners passing back and forth through the channel. On several occasions it was hit by much larger vessels, but it always survived.

In 1932 it was pulled off the Ambrose Channel station and relegated to service as a relief lightship. In 1936, however, the *Ambrose* was reassigned to the crucial Scotland station just off Sandy Hook, New Jersey, where it served until 1964. That year the old lightship went into semiretirement and was given the honor of representing the Coast Guard as an exhibit at the 1964 New York World's Fair.

Since 1968 the *Ambrose* has delighted children and fascinated adults as a key attraction of the South Street Seaport Museum in New York City. The *Ambrose* is a maritime exhibit of particular historical interest. Originally, the lamps atop its main mast and foremast were lit with oil and its engines powered by steam. Eventually its lamps were converted to electricity and its engines to diesel power.

HOW TO GET THERE: *By car, follow FDR Drive on Manhattan's East Side to the Brooklyn Bridge and Civic Center exit, which will place you on Water and Pearl Streets, just 3 blocks north of the South Street Seaport Museum. From the West Side drive around the southern toe of Manhattan through the Battery Park underpass to South Street and the museum. The museum complex is open daily all year long. Admission is charged for most exhibits, including the Ambrose. For hours, special events, and other information, call (212) 748-8600.*

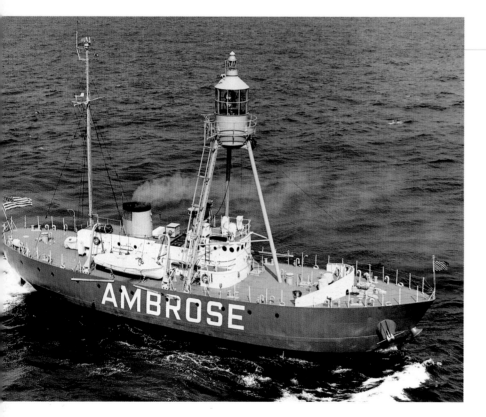

Lightship Number 87 *heads for the Ambrose Channel leading to New York City. Reaching its appointed station, the little lighthouse would drop anchor and maintain its lonely vigil for months at a time. Notice the lantern held aloft by a tripod-type mast. (Courtesy U.S. Coast Guard)*

HUDSON RIVER LIGHTHOUSES

Rondout Creek (Kingston) — 1838 AND 1915

Saugerties — 1836 AND 1869

Esopus Meadows — 1879

Hudson City — 1874

The Hudson River once had as many lighthouses as some entire coastal states have. One of the best known of these marks the harbor entrance of the inland port city of Kingston. The first light station was established here in 1838, but the current 52-foot-square brick tower and attached dwelling date to 1915. Known as the **Rondout Creek Lighthouse,** it stands on a concrete pier surrounded by the river's swirling waters. The Hudson River Maritime Museum has leased the building for use as a museum dedicated to the lives of river lighthouse keepers and their families.

Floodwaters and ice were always a problem for lighthouses on the Hudson. The **Saugerties Lighthouse,** established in 1836, took the beating for nearly thirty years before finally succumbing during the 1860s. The two-story brick dwelling and attached tower that replaced it in 1869 were built on a massive stone caisson meant to shield it from the river's destructive floes. This strategy succeeded, and the lighthouse remained safe and relatively dry until the station was decommissioned eighty-five years later.

Rising from a granite pier near the middle of the heavily trafficked Hudson River, **Esopus Meadows Lighthouse** has withstood more than a century of battering storms, high water, and winter ice floes. Built in 1879, it replaced an earlier structure that had been smashed to bits by ice. During the late 1960s the Coast Guard decommissioned the lighthouse, replacing it with a light on a nearby steel tower. Now under restoration by the Saugerties Lighthouse Conservancy, the old light station can be reached only by boat.

It's a rare thing for a major navigational light to shine more than 100 miles from the nearest expanse of open water. This can be said, however, of the **Hudson City Light.** In fact, not one but two mountain ranges, the Catskills and Berkshires, stand between this lighthouse and the sea.

Established in 1874 to mark the dangerous Middle Ground Flats near the inland port cities of Hudson and Athens, New York, the Hudson City Light still guides shipping to this day. The flats have scarred or breached the hulls of more than one river freighter and barge.

The brick dwelling and 48-foot tower stand on a limestone pier that protects the structure from ice floes. The tower is topped by a small, octagonal

Established in 1838, the Rondout Creek Lighthouse was one of the first navigational beacons on the Upper Hudson. (William Kaufhold)

Built in 1869, the existing Saugerties Lighthouse guided Hudson River pilots for more than eighty years, but after the light was deactivated in 1954, the venerable structure began to deteriorate. In 1986 the Saugerties Lighthouse Conservancy acquired the building, restored it, and eventually relit the beacon. Today the lighthouse is open year-round as a bed-and-breakfast and features a small museum.

lantern room, which once held a fifth-order Fresnel lens. Today the light is automated, and the building is maintained by a local conservation organization dedicated to preserving the old lighthouse.

While winter ice was always a threat to lighthouses and other structures along the river, it also provided seasonal income for many hard-working laborers along this stretch of the Hudson. The thick, clear river ice was sawed into enormous blocks and stored in insulated warehouses for sale during warm-weather months. During the late nineteenth and early twentieth centuries, this Hudson River bounty kept iceboxes cold and rattled in the drink glasses of sweltering city dwellers every summer.

HOW TO GET THERE: *Rondout Creek Lighthouse: Kingston can be reached by way of I–87 (the New York Thruway) or Route 9. For museum hours contact the Hudson River Maritime Museum at (845) 338–0071.*

Saugerties Lighthouse: Handsomely restored by the Saugerties Lighthouse Conservancy, the lighthouse is now a museum and open to the public on weekends. The conservancy is involved in the preservation of other lighthouses as well. Contact the organization at (845) 247–0656.

Esopus Meadows Lighthouse: Down river a few miles from Kingston, the 1879 Esopus Meadows Lighthouse is under restoration by local preservationists. Located in midchannel it cannot be reached from land but can be seen from points along Route 9 on the east side of the river.

Hudson City Light: Well to the north of Saugerties and more than 100 miles from the sea, the Hudson City Lighthouse is located midchannel in the river. This means it cannot be reached from land, but it can be seen from either Hudson City on Route 9 or Athens on Route 385.

Located in the middle of the ice-prone Hudson, Esopus Meadows Lighthouse was placed on a raised platform to protect it from winter ice floes. (William Kaufhold)

The Hudson City Light guards the Middle Ground Flats, a series of dangerous Hudson River shallows that have claimed many barges and other river vessels. (Bob and Sandra Shanklin)

Cape May

CHAPTER TWO

LIGHTS OF THE LONG SANDY SHORE

New Jersey

WHILE THE U.S. LIGHTHOUSE SERVICE, established in 1789, struggled to improve and expand the nation's system of navigational lights, most of the country's coastline remained in the dark. Approximately two dozen lighthouses were in service by 1800, but along vast stretches of often-treacherous shoreline, ships' captains could depend only upon their own skills and instincts for guidance.

Ships nearing the coast were in especially desperate straits when caught in a gale. With no lights to guide them, crews dared not make a run for safe harbor for fear of striking a shoal or having their vessel thrown up on some low, unseen headland and pounded to pieces by breakers. Usually, their only choice was to attempt to ride out the storm. Often they and their ships were swallowed up by the sea and never heard from again.

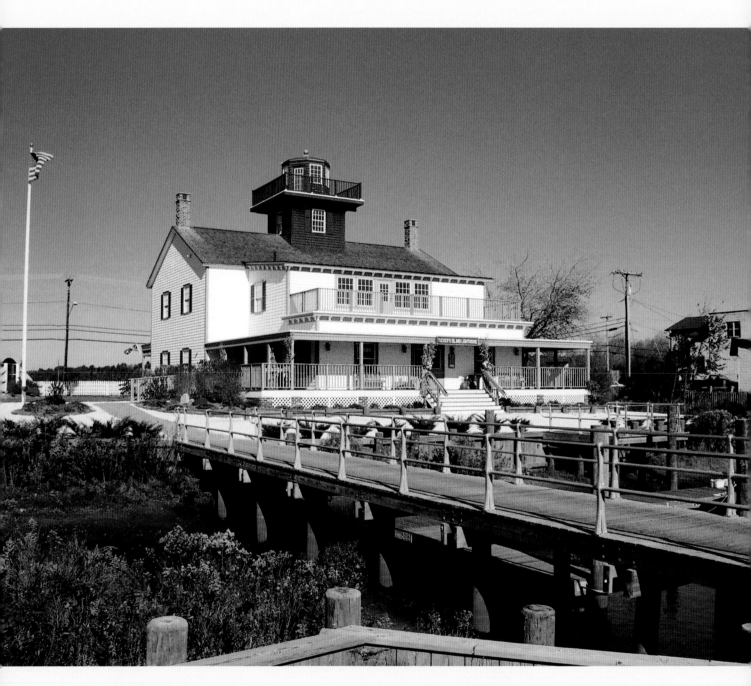

The original Tucker Island Lighthouse was undercut by erosion and collapsed into the sea in 1927. This replica of the old sentinel now serves as an interpretive center at Tuckerton Seaport in southern New Jersey. (H. Kent Edwards)

Hurricanes and nor'easters strike the Mid-Atlantic coast frequently. During the 1800s, when there were no radar or satellites in the sky to track them, these fierce storms appeared without warning. Capable of smashing whole fleets, they often devastated shipping along several hundred miles of coast. The following is only one of the countless maritime calamities caused by these titanic storms.

THE LAST DAYS OF THE *ROSE-IN-BLOOM*

On August 16, 1806, the *Rose-in-Bloom,* a handsomely outfitted ship of commerce, set sail from Charleston, South Carolina, bound for New York City. Among the forty-nine passengers and crew were several notables, including Congressman John Rutledge and the eminent General Joseph MacPherson, who was accompanied by his daughter, Eliza. Once outside the Charleston Harbor, Captain Stephen Barber, a shipmaster of many years' experience, pointed the bow of his ship confidently northward toward New York. It was a voyage he had successfully completed many times before.

By the morning of Friday, August 22, the *Rose-in-Bloom* had made only modest headway and stood just to the northeast of Cape Hatteras. Captain Barber had been fighting unfavorable winds for days and was keeping an eye on the weather. He did not like what he saw—black thunderheads, streaked by lightning, were boiling up out of the southeast. By midday the gale overtook the ship, and it quickly became apparent that this was no ordinary storm.

Before long the winds had torn the sails to shreds. Barber turned the bow into the wind and attempted to heave to under a lone topsail. The *Rose-in-Bloom* held its own for a time, but the topsail was soon ripped away, leaving the ship to drift and wallow helplessly in the towering waves. For nearly two days the wind drove the ship northward. Then, on Sunday morning, she capsized.

Trapped belowdecks, some of the passengers and crew perished immediately. Others scrambled out through gangways, portholes, and skylights to take refuge on the hull. Eventually, muscular crewmen were able to cut away the masts with axes, and the ship slowly righted itself. But the *Rose-in-Bloom* was now a shattered hulk, little better than a raft. Heavy seas constantly swept over the deck, carrying away the weak or unwary. Passenger Benjamin Booth had his wife and infant son torn from his arms and washed into the sea. During the night MacPherson died of cold and exposure. As he died he begged Rutledge to save his daughter. But no one on the broken ship thought that they would ever see land again.

Help was on the way, however. Sailing southward from New Brunswick, the brig *Swift,* under the command of Captain Richard Phelan, had slammed into the same storm that doomed the *Rose-in-Bloom.* It seemed to Phelan and his crew a tempest of almost magical power, an evil storm that brought with it a sulphurous odor, as if the wind were the devil's own breath. For two days the captain and his men fought to hold the *Swift* together as huge waves tossed the brig about like a cork. Then, on Sunday evening, as quickly as it had blown up out of the south to engulf them, the gale subsided.

Phelan reckoned his position to be somewhere off Barnegat, New Jersey, although there wasn't a lighthouse at Barnegat yet to make him certain of his whereabouts.

After sunrise on Monday, August 25, Phelan noticed wreckage floating in the water and soon afterward spotted the remains of the *Rose-in-Bloom.* The ship was obviously about to sink. Survivors aboard the wreck called out desperately for assistance. Although the wind was calm, mountainous waves still rocked and tossed both vessels. Despite the heavy seas, Phelan and volunteers from the *Swift* made several trips in a jolly boat to rescue all who remained alive on the wreck. Not long after the last survivors were pulled to safety, the *Rose-in-Bloom* slipped beneath the waves. Among those who watched the sinking from the *Swift* were Barber, the grieving Booth, and Rutledge, perhaps with his arm around Eliza. In all, twenty-one survived the wreck of the *Rose-in-Bloom.* Twenty-eight others perished.

SANDY HOOK LIGHT

Sandy Hook, New Jersey — 1764

On the evening of June 11, 1764, a keeper trudged up the steps of the recently completed Sandy Hook Lighthouse and lit its lamps for the first time. Today, nearly two-and-a-half centuries later, the light at the very top of the old tower still burns each night. It is not America's first lighthouse—that honor goes to the Boston Lighthouse, established in 1716 and destroyed by the British in 1779—but it is the nation's oldest still standing and operating navigational aid.

Although located in New Jersey, the Sandy Hook Light was known for many years as the New York Lighthouse. Indeed, it was built and paid for by New Yorkers. Weary of losing commerce to better-marked harbors at Boston and elsewhere, a group of New York merchants petitioned their colonial council for a lighthouse. The New York Assembly then held a lottery to raise money and hired Isaac Conro to build a tower near the mouth of the Hudson. To defray the costs of maintenance and pay the keeper's salary, the assembly levied a tax of twenty-two pence per ton on ships arriving at the Port of New York.

When completed, Conro's handiwork was described as follows: "This House is of an Octogan Figure, having eight equal sides; the Diameter of the Base 29 feet; and at the Top of the Wall 15 feet. The Lanthorn is 7 feet high; the Circumference 15 feet. The whole Construction of the Lanthorn is Iron; the Top covered with Copper. There are 48 Oil Blazes. The Building from the Surface is Nine Stories; the whole from Bottom to Top 103 feet." The dimensions of the tower remain roughly the same today.

After the Revolutionary War the Sandy Hook Light precipitated a different sort of war. Since the lighthouse was located in New Jersey but owned by New York, the two states fell into a heated dispute over control of the station. The verbal and legal squabbling continued for years, until the U.S. government finally put an end to the almost-comical conflict in 1790 by making the Sandy Hook station and other lighthouses a federal responsibility.

When the Lighthouse Board began its massive effort during the 1850s to rebuild and modernize America's outdated light stations, inspectors were sent to see if the Sandy Hook tower would need to be replaced. Their report on the board is a compliment to the work done by Conro almost a century earlier: "The tower at Sandy Hook main light was constructed in 1764 under royal charter, of rubblestone, and is now in a good state of preservation. Neither leaks nor cracks were observed in it. The mortar appeared to be good, and it was stated that the annual repairs upon this tower amount to a smaller sum than in towers of any of the minor lights in the New York District."

The board did decide to replace the reflectors in the lantern with a third-order Fresnel lens. Its focal plane 88 feet above the water, the old lens still guides ships into the Hudson with a fixed white light visible from about 19 miles away.

HOW TO GET THERE: *Take Route 36 to Highlands Beach, enter Sandy Hook National Park, and follow the signs to the lighthouse. Still owned and maintained by the Coast Guard, the lighthouse can be approached for viewing. For current information call the Sandy Hook National Park at (732) 872–0115.*

William Kaufhold

NAVESINK LIGHTS

Highlands, New Jersey — 1828 AND 1861

The twin rubblestone towers atop the Navesink Highlands, just south of Sandy Hook, stand among the most historic lighthouses in the United States. Navigational lights shined from this bold headland for almost two centuries, and uncounted thousands of mariners owe the safety of their ships and their very lives to the guidance that these lights provided.

Rising some 200 feet above sea level, the highlands themselves have always served as a natural day mark. Long before the first lights were established here during the mid-1700s, the hills were observed and noted in the logs of European explorers who passed along what is now the northern New Jersey coast. One such adventurous navigator was Henry Hudson, who sailed his ship *Half-Moon* out of the misty waters off Sandy Hook Bay on September 2, 1609. Hudson and his crew saw a series of "high hills" rising from the mists. When the weather cleared enough for them to move in for a closer look, they discovered "a very good land to fall with and a pleasant land to see."

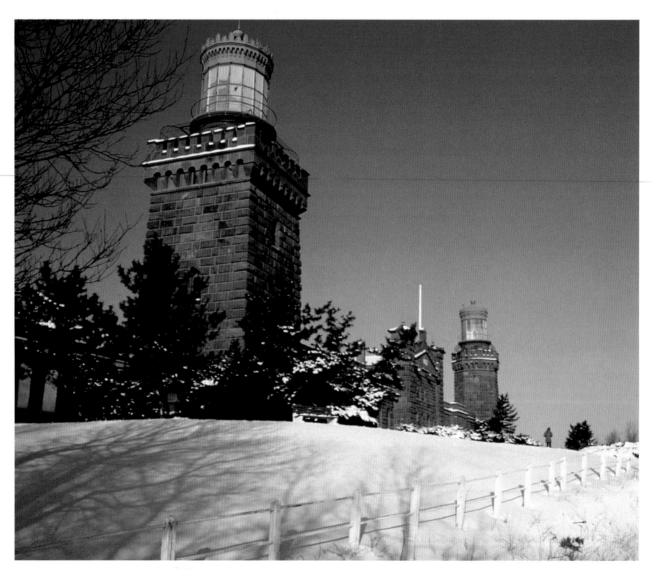

The fortresslike appearance of Navesink Lighthouse belies its peaceful mission. The twin-towered light station guided freighter traffic in and out of the Hudson River from 1828 until 1953. (William Kaufhold)

Many others also found these lands pleasant, as New Jersey and New York grew into prosperous colonies, with bustling ports near the mouth of the Hudson River. To protect these ports from raids by enemy fleets, the colonists established an early warning station at Navesink. Whenever a likely hostile fleet was sighted, a beacon was lighted to alert colonists and their militia as far away as New York City. Ironically, the first Navesink lighthouse was meant as a warning to landward folk rather than to ships and seamen.

A true navigational light is believed to have been in operation here as early as 1756. The light is mentioned in some documents dating to the Revolutionary War, but little else is known about it.

With American independence came a burgeoning of shipping traffic in and out of the Hudson. To help guide these ships, the Navesink Lighthouse was built in 1828. A matched pair of stone towers standing 320 feet apart placed the focal plane of the two lights more than 240 feet above sea level.

Government officials considered this to be among the best and most useful light stations in the country. In fact, the Navesink station was considered so important to maritime commerce that the nation's first Fresnel lenses were installed in its towers. In 1838 Commodore Matthew Perry sailed for France, where he purchased a pair of the advanced prismatic lenses (one first order and one second order) and had them shipped to America. By 1841 the big Fresnels were shining powerfully from the twin Navesink towers.

Several other firsts were associated with the Navesink Lighthouse. It was the first in America to have lamps fueled by kerosene (1883). The first electrically powered seacoast light shined from the south tower beginning in 1898. (By that time an electric navigational light was already in use at the Statue of Liberty, but it served only as a harbor light.)

In 1899 the Navesink Highlands became the site of another first that had profound significance for navigation and for human progress. Employing a transmitter and mast located not far from the light station, Guglielmo Marconi conducted the first practical demonstration of his wireless telegraph. Using the air rather than a wire to carry the electronic dots and dashes, Marconi relayed the results of the America's Cup races off Sandy Hook.

The fortresslike brownstone towers seen today at Navesink date to 1861: They replaced the earlier

The north tower of the Navesink Lighthouse resembles a chessboard rook.

structure at the beginning of the American Civil War. By 1898 the government no longer saw a need for two lights here. It snuffed out the lamp in the north tower. The powerful south light, which could be seen from 22 miles at sea, served until 1953, when it, too, was discontinued. Today the station is part of Twin Lights Historic Site, administered by the New Jersey State Park Service.

HOW TO GET THERE: *To reach the Twin Lights Historic Site, take exit 117 off the Garden State Parkway and follow Highway 36 to Highlands and the museum parking lot. A Fresnel lens can be seen at the museum, which features displays recounting the rich history of the station. Visitors may also tour the nearby Spermacetti Cove life-saving station. For hours and other information, call (732) 872–1814.*

SEA GIRT LIGHT

Sea Girt, New Jersey — 1896

With its weathered brick walls, pitched roof, and spacious balustered porch, the Sea Girt Lighthouse looks much like the other homes and summer cottages in this seaside community. Unlike neighboring houses, however, this one wraps around two sides of a square, 40-foot tower with a gallery and small lantern room perched on top.

This homey-looking lighthouse was built in 1896 to guide fishing boats and other vessels into the shallow Sea Girt Inlet. The light also filled in a dark stretch along the coast between Barnegat Lighthouse, 26 miles to the south, and the twin Navesink Lights, some 19 miles north. The lighthouse accomplished its tasks with a fourth-order Fresnel lens displaying a flashing red light.

In 1917 the Lighthouse Service began experimenting with radio beacons to help guide ships in fog and stormy weather. A pair of transmitters on the New York area lightships *Ambrose* and *Fire Island* and a third at Sea Girt enable navigators to pinpoint their locations through a process of triangulation. The system was eventually adopted worldwide.

The Coast Guard discontinued the Sea Girt Light in 1945 and sold the property to the town. During the 1980s the building was handsomely restored, with funds raised by the Sea Girt Lighthouse Citizens Committee. Today the Sea Girt Light shines again as a private aid to naviation.

HOW TO GET THERE: *From the Garden State Parkway just south of I–195, take the Highway 35 exit and drive south for approximately 6 miles. Then take Route 71 north to Sea Girt, turn right on Beacon Boulevard, and follow it to the lighthouse, which is located in a pleasant residential neighborhood. Visitors are welcome.*

William Kaufhold

William Kaufhold

BARNEGAT LIGHTHOUSE

Long Beach Island, New Jersey — 1835 AND 1859

The man who built the first lighthouse on New Jersey's Barnegat Inlet was none other than Winslow Lewis, a key figure in the early history of the American lighthouse establishment. A retired sea captain, Lewis held a patent on the Argand lamp and parabolic reflector system used in many American lighthouses until the 1850s. A friend of Treasury Department Fifth Auditor and lighthouse czar Stephen Pleasonton, Lewis often won contracts to build and equip light stations.

Lewis's 45-foot Barnegat Inlet tower stood for only about twenty years before a Lighthouse Board inspector found it to be poorly constructed, in a woeful state of disrepair, and hopelessly inadequate for service as a seacoast light. In truth, the board did not think much of Lewis's reflectors, either; it was busy replacing hundreds of them with the vastly more effective Fresnel lenses made by the French.

The inspector who gave the lighthouse its bad report was Lieutenant George Meade. The lieutenant found that Lewis had used decidedly inferior materials in the tower. Mortar crumbled from between bricks, and just below the lantern, a wall bulged out and seemed about to fall. Even if it were repaired, the stubby Lewis tower would serve as little more than an inlet light. Meade felt that the station was strategically located and deserved a more powerful light, with a range sufficient to guide ships at sea. He concluded that the board had little choice but to replace the collapsing structure with a much taller and better-built tower.

Meade's point of view got plenty of support from mariners. Almost from the moment it went into service in 1835, captains complained about the weakness of the light. Some said it was often "impossible to tell whether it is a ship's light or a lighthouse."

Mail steamer Captain H. K. Davenport described the light as "indifferent."

Acting on Meade's advice, the board erected a soaring tower, its lantern room perched 163 feet above the inlet. Fitted with a first-order Fresnel lens, the tower exhibited its powerful new light for the first time on January 1, 1859, and the station entered a new era as a true seacoast light. The nation was about to enter a new era as well. Only a few years after his visit to Barnegat in 1855, lighthouse inspector Meade would serve his country in a very different and significant way. As General Meade, he commanded the Army of the Potomac during the last years of the Civil War.

Deactivated shortly before the end of World War II, the Barnegat Lighthouse might have fallen into ruin and eventually toppled into the Atlantic. Fortunately, lighthouse lovers and the State of New Jersey came to its rescue.

Although inactive as a maritime light for more than half a century, the lighthouse now serves as the main attraction of a popular state park. Nowadays the tower is known affectionately to many locals as "Old Barney."

HOW TO GET THERE: *Take Route 72 to Long Beach Island and follow the signs to Barnegat Lighthouse State Park. Along the way you'll pass through Surf City, North Beach, Harvey Cedars, and Loveladies. Continue to Long Beach Island, turn left, and drive to Barnegat Lighthouse State Park at the far northern end of the island. For a small fee visitors may climb "Old Barney" and enjoy the extraordinary view from the top. The station's big first-order Fresnel lens is on display in the lighthouse museum located in a small nearby schoolhouse. For hours and other park information, call (602) 494–2096.*

ABSECON LIGHTHOUSE
Atlantic City, New Jersey — **1857**

Nowadays vacationers who travel to Atlantic City to enjoy its sparkling oceanside resorts may be mesmerized by the flashing lights of the big casinos. But for much of its early history, this stretch of the Atlantic shoreline was mostly dark at night. Despite the threat of shoals and shallows lurking just offshore, there was no light to warn ships of the danger.

Dr. Jonathan Pitney, looked upon by many as the founder of Atlantic City, fought a lifelong battle with federal authorities to have a lighthouse constructed at this site. Unfortunately for Dr. Pitney, his efforts ran aground on the stubbornness of Fifth Auditor Stephen Pleasonton, the tightfisted Treasury Department bureaucrat who presided over the U.S. Lighthouse Service as if it were his own medieval fiefdom. Pitney confronted Pleasonton with stacks of reports detailing New Jersey shore shipwrecks going all the way back to the 1700s. Despite the evidence, the fifth auditor maintained that there was no money for a midcoast New Jersey lighthouse—and scant need of one.

It was only after Pleasonton lost his grip on the service when Congress created the Lighthouse Board during the early 1850s that the Abescon project finally got under way. It would be one of three New Jersey lighthouses built at about that time, the others being Barnegat and Cape May. All three of these impressive structures are slender towers in excess of 170 feet tall.

The area around what is now Atlantic City was orginally called Absegame after the Indian tribe that once lived in this area. For the new lighthouse to be built here, officials selected a slightly corrupted version of the same name: Absecon. In August 1854 Congress appropriated $35,000 for the Absecon project, and work was soon begun.

It was slow going, however; water from a nearby salt marsh kept filling the foundation pit. Crews tried bucket brigades and manned hand pumps, but to no avail. Eventually, a newfangled steam pump was successfully applied to the task, and workers were able to pour the foundation. Then the money ran out. Only after Congress coughed up an additional $17,000 could work be completed.

Supervising the last stages of construction was Major George G. Meade, a little-known U.S. Army engineer. Only a few years later, he would be better known as General Meade, commander of the Union Army of the Potomac. In 1863 Meade managed another carefully engineered undertaking—the Union victory at Gettysburg.

Fitted with a state-of-the-art, first-order Fresnel lens, the Absecon Light was at long last ready for service by early 1857, and keeper Daniel Scull first lit its whale-oil lamps on January 15 of that year. The light would burn each night, more or less without interruption, for more than sixty-five years.

Its career, however, could have been much shorter. During the 1870s the ocean threatened to destroy the tower by cutting away its foundation. The tower had been built a quarter of a mile from the nearest ocean waves, but by 1876 storm-driven erosion had brought the Atlantic within two dozen yards of the foundation.

Engineers put forward several plans for saving the lighthouse. One of the least probable of these called for lifting the enormous tower onto rails and moving it a mile inland—all for only $10,000 and supposedly without missing a single night of service. Officials chose a simpler and more likely solution, that of building a long jetty to block the path of the eroding sand.

So successful was the jetty, completed in 1878, that, within two years, the ocean had pulled back more than 1,300 feet to its original distance from the lighthouse.

Although the Absecon Lighthouse won its tug-of-war with the ocean, it eventually succumbed to progress. By the early twentieth century, what had once been a lonely coastal village had grown into a bustling city. Buildings obscured the beacon, and mariners could not distinguish it from the bright lights of Atlantic City.

In 1933 the Coast Guard discontinued the light and deeded the tower to the city. It still stands today, among the tallest of Atlantic City's many brightly lit attractions.

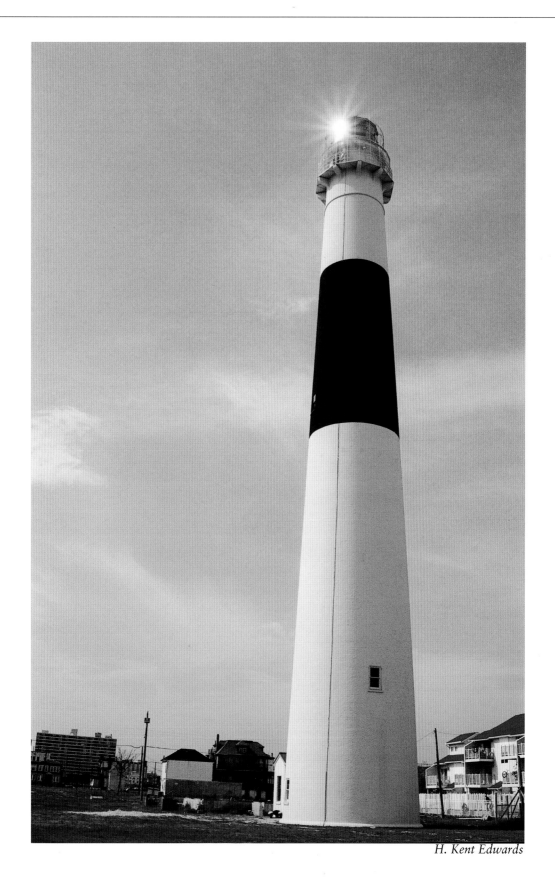

H. Kent Edwards

HOW TO GET THERE: *Located at the intersection of Rhode Island and Pacific Avenues in Atlantic City, the Absecon Lighthouse was handsomely restored during the 1960s. Restoration work is once more under way.*

Visitors will find a gift shop and museum in the reconstructed keeper's residence. For additional information call (609) 449–1360.

HEREFORD INLET LIGHT

North Wildwood, New Jersey — 1874

A lovely structure of considerable architectural interest, the Hereford Inlet Lighthouse was built in 1873–74 by the Army Corps of Engineers. A stick-style frame building, with a long porch, delicate balusters, and a four-story square tower pushing up through the center of a pitched roof, its fanciful appearance strongly suggests the Victorian era that produced it. Oddly enough, this seemingly unique structure has a near twin, the Point Fermin Lighthouse, built at about the same time in Southern California.

Completed at a relatively modest cost of $25,000, this unusual lighthouse was nonetheless a sturdy piece of work. Lieutenant Colonel W. F. Reynolds, the army engineer who had also supervised construction of the massive Barnegat tower farther to the north, made sure that the Hereford Inlet Lighthouse had the solid construction necessary to stand up to Atlantic storms.

In 1889 a hurricane crashed into the coast of southern New Jersey, drowning many coastal residents and driving thousands from their homes. Among those who counted themselves lucky were eighteen people who took refuge in the Hereford Inlet Lighthouse. The building was soon surrounded by turbulent waters. Although shaken by high wind and pounded by waves, the lighthouse and its frightened guests survived.

Despite storms and a couple of nearly disastrous fires, the Hereford Inlet Lighthouse remained in service for ninety years. Discontinued by the Coast Guard in 1964, it was replaced by a far less attractive, skeleton-type tower. The grounds were transferred to the State of New Jersey and the building boarded up to thwart vandals. So it sat until 1986, when the citizens of North Wildwood successfully petitioned the Coast Guard and received permission to reopen the lighthouse and operate it privately as an aid to navigation.

In recent years, extensive restoration work and a fresh paint job have returned Hereford Inlet Lighthouse to its original appearance. (H. Kent Edwards)

HOW TO GET THERE: *Near the far south end of the Garden State Parkway, take the Route 147 exit and drive east toward the Atlantic into North Wildwood. The lighthouse stands just off Central Avenue, between Chestnut and First Streets, and is open during the summer. The keeper's residence houses a maritime museum and the station's 1874 Fresnel lens. For hours and other information, call (609) 522–4520.*

CAPE MAY LIGHT

Cape May Point, New Jersey — 1824, 1847, AND 1859

At 157½ feet tall, the tower of the Cape May Lighthouse soars above the flat, sandy New Jersey coastline and the blue Atlantic beyond. Built in 1859, the distinctive white tower still guides shipping along the coast and into Delaware Bay. The enormous tower replaced two earlier structures dating to 1824 and 1847, respectively.

Exactly 199 steps lead from the ground floor to the lantern room. The focal plane of the extraordinary 600,000-candlepower beacon is 165 feet above sea level.

While the light is still active, it has been automated; most of the outbuildings and the keepers' dwellings are no longer in use. The keepers' houses are currently under restoration.

According to local tradition (and to rangers at Cape May Point State Park), the old lighthouse has a certain strong influence on young lovers. More than one proposal of marriage has been made—and accepted—atop the tower.

HOW TO GET THERE: *Follow the Garden State Parkway south until it ends at Cape May. Take Route 109 south and then Lafayette Street almost to the Atlantic. Then turn right onto Sunset Boulevard and follow it to Lighthouse Avenue. Turn right and enter Cape May Point State Park. There is a small admission fee to the lighthouse. For current park hours and fees, call (609) 884–5404.*

LIGHTHOUSES OF DELAWARE BAY

Brandywine Shoal — 1828, 1850, AND 1914
Ship John Shoal — 1877
Fourteen-Foot Shoal — 1888
Miah Maull — 1913

mong the most important and historic waterways in America, the Delaware Bay and Delaware River link Wilmington, Philadelphia, Trenton, and other key inland cities to the Atlantic. Unfortunately, nature has strewn this vital maritime highway with dangerous obstructions, forcing vessels to run a gauntlet of shoals and shallows. Several particularly threatening obstacles have been marked with lighthouses.

As long ago as the 1820s, efforts were made to mark the deadly Brandywine Shoal near Lewes, but the open-water lighthouse built here in 1828 could not stand up to the pummeling it took from howling gales and nor'easters. A lightship took its place until 1850, when the **Brandywine Shoal Lighthouse** was built atop a forest of piles driven directly into the bottom of the bay. This innovative design was in part the brainchild of George Meade, a military engineer who would later lead the Union Army to victory at Gettysburg. The pile technique proved successful, and the 1850 lighthouse served until shortly before World War I, when it was replaced by the caisson structure that still guards the shoal.

Although pile construction provided an effective and low-cost means of marking shallow water channels and obstacles, lighthouses of this type were vulnerable to ice floes and storm-driven waves. As at Brandywine Shoal, most pile lighthouses were eventually replaced by sturdier caisson light stations placed on massive iron cylinders filled with rock or concrete. Built in 1877, the **Ship John Shoal Light** near the entrance to the Delaware River was among America's first caisson-style lighthouses. With its Victorian mansard roof, it is remarkably old fashioned in appearance, but its guiding light is no less effective than when the station was established more than one and a quarter century ago. Not far from the Ship John Shoal Light, another caisson lighthouse marks Fourteen Foot Shoal near Bowers Beach. Established in 1888, the **Fourteen-Foot Shoal Lighthouse** features a squared-off cast-iron tower and dwelling.

Built in 1828, Brandywine Shoal is the oldest of several Delaware Bay lighthouses. (H. Kent Edwards)

Originally these Delaware Bay lighthouses were equipped with Fresnel lenses and maintained by full-time crews. The keepers were all removed years ago when the stations were automated, and all but one of the old Fresnels have been replaced by modern optics—now powered by batteries recharged with solar panels. The **Miah Maull Lighthouse** is the exception. Completed in 1913 atop a hefty caisson out near the center of the bay, its 45-foot tower retains its original fourth-order Fresnel lens.

HOW TO GET THERE: *These open-water structures are best seen from a boat. For information on access or occasional tours, call the Delaware River & Bay Lighthouse Foundation at (302) 644–7046.*

The **Ship John Shoal Lighthouse** *(top right) was named after a vessel that ran aground here in 1797 (H. Kent Edwards). Built in 1913, the* **Miah Maull Shoal Lighthouse** *(below) was the last offshore light station established in Delaware Bay (H. Kent Edwards).* **The Fourteen-Foot Shoal Lighthouse** *(bottom right) takes its name from the depth of the water over the shoal it marks (Courtesy U.S. Coast Guard).*

Baltimore Harbor Light (© Mark Riddick/New Light Photography)

CHAPTER THREE

LIGHTS OF THE BIG BAYS

Delaware and Maryland

MUCH LIKE THE SHIPS and sailors who depend on them, lighthouses are perishable. Many of the nation's earliest lighthouses disappeared long ago. Storms bowled them over, or floods and beach erosion cut away their foundations, causing them to topple into the sea. A few were cut down by cannonballs, explosives, and other weapons of war. A surprising number fell victim to the same people who had them built in the first place—members of the Lighthouse Service or Coast Guard who pulled them down to make way for newer, supposedly better navigational facilities. Many others simply grew old and fell down from neglect.

After guiding generations of mariners, the Hooper Strait Lighthouse was slated for demolition in 1966. Instead, it was cut in half like an apple and barged to St. Michaels, Maryland, where it was reassembled for use as a museum exhibit.

Whenever a lighthouse is destroyed, America loses part of its heritage, a reminder of the often-heroic struggles of the past. But not all vanished lighthouses are lost forever. Indeed, some are eventually rebuilt by the government or by local societies for use as museums. Others continue to be celebrated in books, songs, and memory. In a few instances, lights that no longer shine are still shown on navigation charts. Some old salts swear that, when the weather is just right, they can see a ghostly light emanating from a point where a demolished lighthouse once stood.

Some fallen lighthouses played too important in the nation's history ever to be forgotten. One such was the Cape Henlopen Lighthouse in Delaware.

SAGA OF THE CAPE HENLOPEN LIGHTHOUSE

The Cape Henlopen Lighthouse was the seventh major light tower built in the original thirteen American colonies. Completed in 1765, it was financed and operated not by the people of Delaware but by those of Pennsylvania. The merchants of Philadelphia made handsome profits on goods brought by ships moving up the Delaware River. Naturally they wanted to make the trip to their bustling wharves as easy and safe as possible.

In a manner that might seem familiar to citizens nowadays, Pennsylvania officials attempted to raise money for the project by means of a lottery. Proceeds of the game fell considerably short of the 7,674 pounds sterling needed for construction, however, so the provincial assembly issued a series of lighthouse bonds, at six percent interest, to make up the difference.

Built at considerably more expense than most other eighteenth-century American lighthouses, the Cape Henlopen tower was made to last. Construction crews used granite brought from quarries upriver near Wilmington, Delaware. Laying the granite down in courses, they gave the tower fortresslike walls, 6 feet thick at the base and 69 feet tall. It had eight interior levels, each with its own window. On the eighth level was the lantern room, glassed in on all sides. A wooden stairway wound around the inner walls of the tower, providing access to the top. The original lamps were fueled by whale oil when it was available and by lard oil at other times. The tower stood on a sandy hill, which boosted the light to a level more then 115 feet above the water. Some captains claimed to have seen it from 17 miles at sea.

Cape Henlopen Light (National Archives)

Pointing the way to prosperous Philadelphia, the Cape Henlopen Lighthouse quickly became one of the most important landmarks in North America. Thousands of British and colonial ships followed its guidance and noted the light in their logs.

It had shone for only a few years, however, when relations between the colonists and their mother country began to sour. By 1775 hostilities seemed inevitable, and the colonists placed a lookout in the Cape Henlopen tower to watch for approaching warships. Should he spot an invasion fleet, the lookout's duty was to ride for Philadelphia hell-for-leather, Paul Revere style, to give the warning.

Instead of an invading armada, the British sent individual warships to harass the colonists. The colonials fought back with a tiny fleet of their own. The young John Paul Jones served aboard one of these small vessels, the *Alfred*. Nonetheless, the British were successful in bottling up the American ships in the Delaware River.

As is the case with many lighthouses now serving as museums, the Drum Point Lighthouse, in Solomons, Maryland, contains many artifacts from an earlier era.

In 1777 the British warship *Roebuck* anchored off the cape. With his ship sorely in need of supplies, the captain sent a party of foragers ashore near the lighthouse to round up some cattle to feed his hungry crew. The Cape Henlopen keeper, a stout-hearted Patriot named Hedgecock, refused to sell his cows. To keep the British from "commandeering" (the military word for stealing) the beasts, he drove them into the woods. Hedgecock threatened to give the British "some bullets" instead of beef. No match for the well-armed raiding party, however, Hedgecock had to take to the woods himself.

Having missed out on a steak dinner, the angry sailors set fire to the lighthouse. Feeding primarily on the wooden staircase, the fire gutted the tower. The light station would not be repaired and back on active duty again until 1784, just after the end of the war.

WHAT SO PROUDLY WE HAILED

A generation afterward, in 1812, Americans were once again at war with the British, and again the Cape Henlopen Light played an important role. During the early months of the war, the light guided U.S. naval vessels in and out of the Delaware. Privateers followed the light into the bay with British prizes that they had captured at sea. But by the spring of 1813, the British had clamped a tight blockade on the Delaware, and American vessels could no longer get in or out.

To strike back at the British and make navigation as dangerous as possible for the blockading fleet, the Americans darkened the Cape Henlopen Light and removed all buoys and markers from the bay. This proved an especially damaging broadside, as time and again British ships slammed into obstacles or ran aground on shoals lurking just beneath the waters of the cape.

The British also had a very hard time obtaining provisions of meat and freshwater. More often than not, foraging parties were greeted with a fusillade of militia bullets. Facing critical shortages, the British sailed their fleet around Cape Henlopen, trained its guns on the town of Lewes, and demanded supplies. Its defenses bolstered by 1,000 militiamen hurried to the cape from the north, the town flung the British demands back at them in the form of musket and cannon shot. The British, in turn, replied with a mighty cannonade that lasted all day. In a Fort McHenry–style bombardment, they pounded the town with more than 800 thirty-two-pound explosive shots. But the marksmanship of the British gunners was poor, and they did very little telling damage. When evening fell, the American flag still fluttered over the town, and the British fleet was forced to withdraw. The proud militia commander reported to his superiors that the British attack had "killed one chicken and wounded a pig."

With the end of the war in 1814, the Cape Henlopen Light returned to its peacetime duties. The old lighthouse, however, was now locked in another battle, one that would last for more than a century and one that it would eventually lose. This time, the enemy was the Atlantic Ocean itself, which was constantly shaping and reshaping the cape. The beach was steadily eroding and the sandy cape retreating in a generally northwesterly direction. By 1884 high tides were approaching the very foundation of the tower.

Alarmed lighthouse officials ordered a series of protective measures. Brush was piled up around the tower and dwelling to trap windblown soil, while piers and bulwarks were built along the beach in an attempt to dam the river of sand flowing to the north. These measures slowed the river but did not stop it.

The Cape Henlopen Light survived to serve in one more international conflict: World War I. Keepers kept an eye out for German submarines thought to be prowling just outside the Delaware Bay. But after the war the lighthouse began to lose its struggle with the sea, as tides cut farther and farther under the sandbank that served as its platform. After major storms sailors looked anxiously to the cape to see if the tower was still there. Its last day came on April 13, 1926, a sunny day with light winds. Shortly after noon the Cape Henlopen tower tumbled down into the sea.

Occasionally, at the last gleam of twilight, sailors on ships off Cape Henlopen report seeing a light emanating from a point near where the old lighthouse once stood. Some say that these mariners have seen the Delaware Breakwater Light, which is often visible from beyond the cape. Others are not so sure, and when the night is especially dark, they scan the western horizon looking for the light that, for more than 150 years, so seldom failed them.

LISTON REAR RANGE LIGHT

Fort Penn, Delaware — 1877 AND 1906

Range lighthouses operate in pairs to mark channels for shipping. Arrayed one behind the other with the rear light on a higher plane, the beacons will be seen in perfect vertical alignment by the pilots of ships sailing safely through the channel. But if the upper light appears to tilt either to the left or right of vertical, the vessel is straying out of the channel in the direction indicated, and a course correction must be made.

Over the years several range lighthouses have served ships moving up through the Delaware Bay toward the bustling port cities of Wilmington and Philadelphia. Perhaps the most remarkable of these is the Liston Rear Range Lighthouse, located near Fort Penn, Delaware.

Most range lighthouse towers are of relatively modest height, but this one is 120 feet tall, and its light has a focal plane more than 175 feet above the waters of the bay. A black metal cylinder supported by a pyramid-shaped steel skeleton, it was built in 1877. Originally, its lofty lantern room held a second-order Fresnel lens. Although the Fresnel was removed when the station was automated in 1976, the airport-style beacon that replaced it can boast five-million candlepower. Located some distance away and closer to the river, the front range tower is 45 feet tall and dates from 1906. Both lights remain in operation.

HOW TO GET THERE: *Take U.S. Highway 13 north from Dover or south from Wilmington and turn eastward onto Route 2. The Liston light station is located less than a mile from Highway 13.*

The Liston Rear Range Light, near Fort Penn, is one of a pair of lights marking the safe channel through Delaware Bay. (© Mark Riddick/New Light Photography)

Although the lightship Overfalls *spent much of its operational life off the rugged coast of New England, the vessel has now found a home on land at Lewes beside the Delaware Bay. When the* Overfalls *was retired in 1973, the Lewes Historical Society acquired the little vessel and restored it for use as a museum. For more information on the lightship* Overfalls, *call (302) 644–8050. (Courtesy U.S. Coast Guard)*

LIGHTS OF THE HARBOR OF REFUGE

Delaware Breakwater — 1885
Harbor of Refuge Breakwater — 1896 AND 1926

Gales, hurricanes, and nor'easters often rip into America's Mid-Atlantic coast, sometimes striking with little or no warning. Vessels caught in a storm along these shores seek any shelter they can find, but safe harbors that can be reached easily from open water are few and far between. That is why, when violent weather approaches, ships often make a run for the mouth of the Delaware River. There they can hope to ride out the fury of a storm in the relatively quiet waters behind the protective barrier of Cape Henlopen.

Recognizing the importance of this area to shipping, the federal government established, during the late nineteenth century, an anchorage just west of Cape Henlopen. Designating it a "National Harbor of Refuge," the government constructed a series of breakwaters to increase the protection offered by the cape. Two of these were marked by lighthouses.

Completed in 1885, the **Delaware Breakwater Lighthouse** was positioned so that its light could be seen from both the harbor and ocean. A second lighthouse, built in 1896, marked the entrance to the Harbor of Refuge. The two breakwater lights served in conjunction with the much stronger beacon of the nearby Cape Henlopen Lighthouse (see pages 54–57). Fitted with an enormous, first-order Fresnel lens, the Cape Henlopen Lighthouse was one of the best-known and most powerful navigational lights in America. Its days were numbered, however; tottering on a foundation seriously weakened by erosion, the 160-year-old Cape Henlopen tower collapsed in April 1926. Instead of rebuilding the old Cape Henlopen tower, lighthouse officials decided to rely on the existing breakwater lights.

Delaware Breakwater Light stands on a concrete-and-stone caisson. To help it stand up to storms, the 49-foot brick tower is encased in iron plates. The lantern room once held a fourth-order Fresnel lens, but this was replaced by an airport-style beacon when the station was automated in 1973.

Damaged by a series of storms, the thirty-year-old tower marking the harbor entrance was abandoned in 1926. It was replaced by the **Harbor of Refuge Breakwater Lighthouse,** built that same year. Located in a caisson at the south end of the outer-harbor breakwater, its cast-iron tower stands 76 feet tall. Originally fitted with a fourth-order Fresnel lens, it was automated in 1973 and given an optic similar to that of its neighbor across the harbor. Both of these breakwater lights remain in operation, serving storm-battered ships in search of a safe harbor.

HOW TO GET THERE: *From U.S. Highway 9 follow Route 18 to Cape Henlopen State Park. The lighthouses can be seen from several points along the main park road. The beaches here are extremely pleasant, and there are plenty of good spots for picnicking. While in the area plan to visit the lightship Overfalls in Lewes; call (302) 644–8050.*

Exposed to the often-violent Atlantic, the Harbor of Refuge Breakwater Lighthouse stands secure atop a massive concrete caisson. (© Mark Riddick/New Light Photography)

Delaware Breakwater Lighthouse
(© Mark Riddick/New Light Photography)

FENWICK ISLAND LIGHT

Fenwick Island, Delaware — 1858

enwick Island Light is actually in Delaware, which was once part of Pennsylvania, but it can be viewed without ever leaving Maryland because the transpeninsular line, an early survey that became part of the Mason-Dixon line, ran through the lighthouse property, separating Delaware and Maryland. In fact, Mr. Mason and Mr. Dixon began their famous survey on Fenwick Island and used the transpeninsular marker, which had been placed years earlier, in 1750, as the start of their famous line between the North and the South.

Built in 1858 to guide ships into Delaware Bay, Fenwick Island Lighthouse is 87 feet tall, with a focal plane of 83 feet above sea level. It holds a third-order Fresnel lens. The first painting of the lighthouse cost the U.S. government exactly $5.00.

The lighthouse is owned by the State of Delaware and is maintained by the nonprofit Friends of Fenwick Island. The lighthouse is open to the public and depends upon private contributions for most of its maintenance.

The light, visible from 15 miles at sea, fills an otherwise dark gap between Assateague Light in Virginia and the Cape Henlopen Lighthouse to the north.

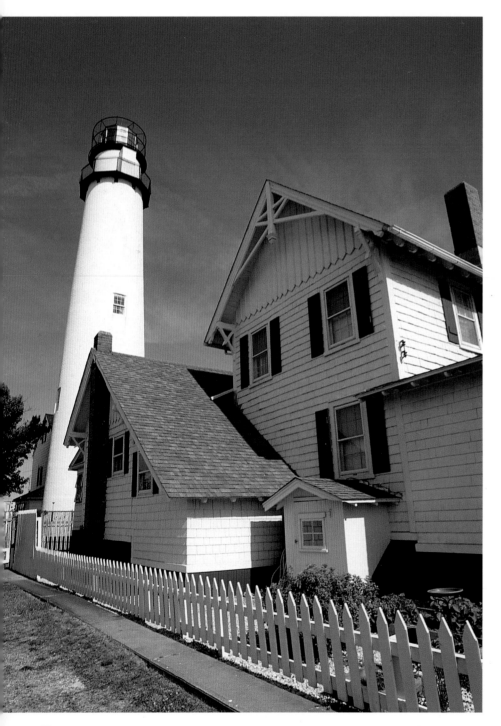

HOW TO GET THERE: *Fenwick Island Light is located 2 blocks west of Route 1 on 146th Street in North Ocean City, Maryland. The tower contains a small museum. For hours and other information, call (302) 436–8410.*

TURKEY POINT LIGHT

Elk Neck, Maryland — 1833

urkey Point juts southward into the Chesapeake Bay near its far north end. A modest masonry light tower has stood here since 1833, its beacon guiding ships headed for the Susquehanna River. Although the tower is only 38 feet tall, it stands on a 100-foot-high bluff, which gives it a considerable boost in height and effectiveness.

The government paid contractor John Donohoo $4,355 to build the tower and nearby keeper's dwelling. Donohoo built a number of Chesapeake lighthouses, including those at Thomas Point, Piney Point, and Point Lookout.

For more than twenty years, the Turkey Point Lighthouse was home to Mrs. Harry Salter, the last female in the nation's corps of civilian keepers. She had received her appointment from President Calvin Coolidge in 1925 after the death of her husband, the previous keeper. Mrs. Salter retired when the station was automated in 1947. Earlier female keepers had served here as well, including Elizabeth Lusby, who kept the light burning from 1844 to 1861, and Clara Blumfield, who held the keeper's post from 1895 to 1919.

The Coast Guard deactivated the Turkey Point Light in 2000. Since that time, a local preservation group known as Turkey Point Light Station, Inc., has taken possession of the property and reestablished the beacon as a private aid to navigation.

HOW TO GET THERE: *Only the lighthouse tower still stands. It is located at the far end of pristine Elk Neck State Park, a major game preserve. The park and lighthouse are accessible to the public via Route 272.*

Follow I–95 north from Baltimore and look for the Route 272 exit several miles past the Susquehanna Bridge. When approaching from Wilmington, Delaware, the Route 272 exit is about 12 miles beyond the Maryland state line.

© *Mark Riddick/New Light Photography*

CONCORD POINT LIGHT

Havre de Grace, Maryland — 1827

Two years after he had built the Thomas Point Lighthouse—and botched the job—John Donohoo won a contract to erect a lighthouse on Concord Point at Havre de Grace. Donohoo completed the 32-foot stone tower in less than a year for $3,500, and this time his work was solid. The tower still stands today, looking very much as it did when its lamps were first lit in 1827.

Originally, the lantern held a set of lamps and 16-inch reflectors. Later these were exchanged for a fifth-order Fresnel lens, among the smallest Fresnels available. Today the tower displays a fixed green light as a private aid to navigation. The light has been automated since the 1920s.

All the keepers of the Concord Point Light came from a single family, that of war hero John O'Niel. During the War of 1812, O'Niel had made a quixotic one-man stand against an entire British fleet. Miraculously, he survived and later was rewarded with the post of keeper at the Concord Point Light. The job was passed down from one generation of O'Niels to the next. Finally, in the 1920s, the light was automated, and great-grandson Harry O'Niel had to surrender the tower key. The beacon remains operational, although it is no longer an official aid to navigation.

HOW TO GET THERE: *Take State 155 off I–95 into Havre de Grace and turn left onto Otsego Street. Then turn right onto Saint John's Street and, finally, left again at the sign for Concord Point. If you get lost, remember that the light is near the Susquehanna River in the southeast part of town. Although hours are limited, the lighthouse is open to the public most weekends and on holidays. For general information contact the town of Havre de Grace at (410) 939–9040; for group tours call (410) 939–1498.*

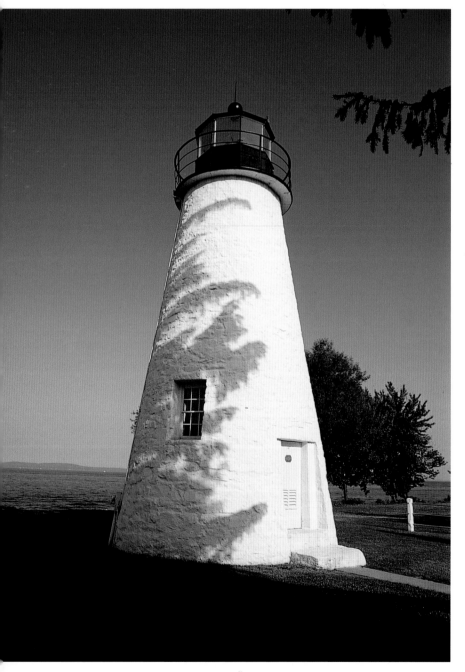

SEVEN FOOT KNOLL LIGHTHOUSE

Baltimore, Maryland — 1855

On August 21, 1933, Maryland was hit by a storm so violent that it destroyed hundreds of homes and boats along the Atlantic coast and in the Chesapeake Bay. Out on the bay, the dark-red, cheese-box-shaped Seven Foot Knoll Lighthouse was torn by 90-mile-per-hour winds and pounded by 15-foot waves. The lighthouse trembled and shook, but keeper Thomas Steinise was sure it would stand up to the beating, just as it had so many times in the past.

Then, above the roar of the wind, he heard a disturbing sound—the high-pitched signal of a vessel in distress. The call came from *Point Breeze,* a tugboat that had been running for the safety of some protective harbor when it was caught and overwhelmed by the waves.

The hapless tug sank within 500 yards of the lighthouse. Facing near-certain death, Steinise lowered the station's 21-foot dory into the chaotic waters and pulled with all his strength for the wreck. For more than two hours, the keeper battled the storm single-handedly in his open boat. He managed to rescue the six crewmen.

For his part in the dramatic rescue, Steinise was awarded the Congressional Medal for heroism. "Just doing what was right," the modest Steinise told reporters.

Seven Foot Knoll is the oldest surviving example of the Chesapeake's classic screw-pile lighthouses. Completed in 1855, it served mariners as an active light or day mark for more than 130 years. Designed for a third-order lens, it received a fourth-order Fresnel instead. During fog and heavy weather, the keeper sounded a bell.

First automated and then put out of service by the Coast Guard, the lighthouse was eventually donated to the City of Baltimore for use as a museum. In 1988 the 220-ton structure was cut from its pilings and carried on a barge to its current location at Pier 5, in the city's popular Inner Harbor district.

HOW TO GET THERE: *From I–95 take the Pratt Street exit and follow the signs to the Baltimore Inner Harbor. There are several parking lots in the area just off Pratt Street. The lighthouse is located near the end of Pier 5. The lightship* Chesapeake *is located nearby. Both the lighthouse and lightship are part of the Baltimore Maritime Museum; call (410) 837–4636. The Baltimore Inner Harbor offers several excellent restaurants and plenty of intriguing shops. The National Aquarium, located near Pier 5, is a must-see.*

LIGHTSHIP *CHESAPEAKE*

Baltimore, Maryland — 1930

With an overall length of 133 feet, a 30-foot beam, and a displacement of only 130 gross tons, the *Chesapeake* is a feisty little vessel. Launched in 1930, she guided ships in and out of Chesapeake Bay until World War II, when German U-boats menaced shipping along the Eastern Seaboard. Fitted with a pair of 20-mm guns, the *Chesapeake* was drafted into the Navy and served out the war as a harbor-patrol boat. Following the war she became a lightship once again and returned to her original duty station.

Decommissioned by the Coast Guard in 1971, the hard-working *Chesapeake* became a seagoing environmental classroom for schoolchildren.

Since 1988, when it was loaned to the City of Baltimore, the ship has provided a different sort of edu-cation. As one of the most popular exhibits at the Baltimore Maritime Museum, it reminds visitors of the historic role of lightships in the nation's history.

HOW TO GET THERE: *From I–95 take the Pratt Street exit and follow the signs to the Baltimore Inner Harbor. Several parking lots are available just off Pratt Street in the Inner Harbor area. The lightship* Chesapeake *is berthed in the harbor near the intersection of Pratt and Gay Streets. Nearby is the USS* Constellation, *one of the nation's early wooden fighting ships. The Baltimore Maritime Museum can be reached at (410) 837–4636.*

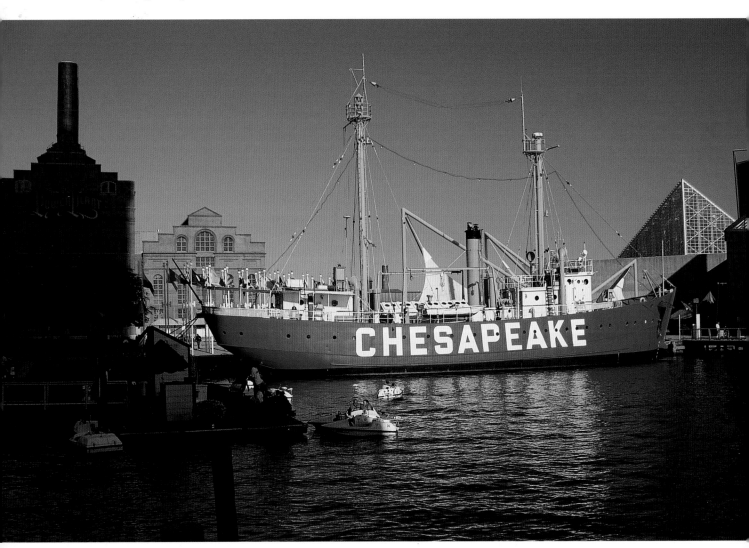

SANDY POINT SHOAL LIGHT

Skidmore, Maryland — 1883

With its mansard roof and pitched dormer windows, the Sandy Shoal Lighthouse looks more like an old Victorian residence than a navigational marker. Its location is distinctly maritime, however, as it is located almost a mile offshore and surrounded by the choppy waters of Chesapeake Bay.

A dangerous shoal extends from Maryland's Sandy Point nearly a mile out into the Chesapeake. Countless vessels have come to grief on this obstacle, which is made all the more threatening by a significant narrowing of the bay between Jones Point on the west and Kent Island to the east. In 1858 the Lighthouse Board established a light station onshore at Sandy Point, but it was of only limited use to pilots trying to avoid the shoal, especially in fog or stormy weather.

After petitioning Congress many times to provide funds for a new and better lighthouse, the board finally secured $25,000 for the project in 1882. Completed the following year, the two-and-a-half-story brick structure stands on a 35-foot-wide, concrete-and-stone caisson at the outer edge of the shoal. A combination dwelling and tower, it rises 50 feet above the waters of the bay. The fanciful design reflects the Victorian era in which it was built. Automated in 1963, the light remains in operation, displaying a white flash ten times every minute.

HOW TO GET THERE: *The Sandy Point Shoal Lighthouse can be reached only by boat and is off-limits to the public. It can be seen to the north as you cross the Chesapeake Bay Bridge; if you are driving, however, please keep your eyes on the road. The best place to view the light is from Sandy Point State Park, accessible from an exit off U.S. Highway 50 just west of the bridge tollbooths. The park is also a great place to have a picnic and enjoy the Chesapeake scenery.*

© *Mark Riddick/New Light Photography*

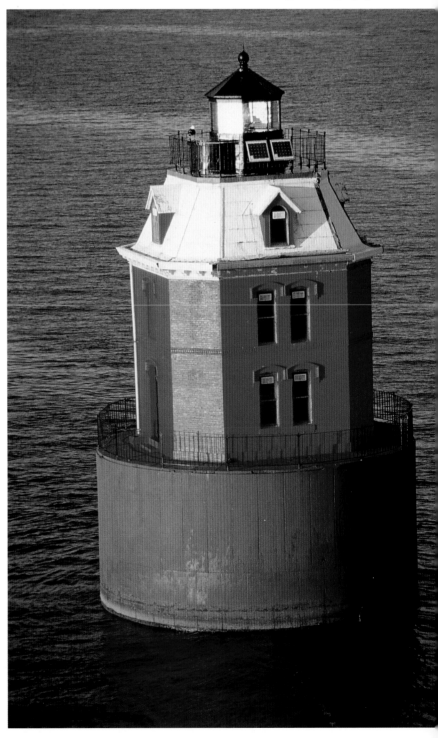

HOOPER STRAIT LIGHTHOUSE
Saint Michaels, Maryland — 1867 AND 1879

For more than forty years, beginning in 1827, the crooked channel of Hooper Strait was marked by a lightship. But in 1867 the Lighthouse Board built a modest screw-pile tower there to guide shipping. Ten years later a massive ice floe swept the little lighthouse off its piles and carried it 5 miles down the bay. A tender found the wreckage and managed to salvage the lens and some of the equipment.

A larger, hexagonal lighthouse had replaced the crushed tower by the autumn of 1879, and it remained in service for three-quarters of a century. Deactivated in 1954, it was eventually acquired by the Chesapeake Bay Maritime Museum in Saint Michaels, on the Maryland eastern shore. In order to move the 44-foot-wide structure down the Chesapeake to Saint Michaels, museum officials had it cut in half, like a giant apple, and loaded onto a barge. Reassembled and restored to like-new condition, the lighthouse now stands beside the museum on Navy Point.

HOW TO GET THERE: *To reach the museum and lighthouse, take U.S. Highway 50 north from Cambridge and then State 33 east to Saint Michaels, a charming Chesapeake Bay community. The museum, which is near the downtown area on Navy Point, is a village in itself, with houses, stores, a restaurant, and wonderful exhibits of small boats used by the bay watermen.*

The lighthouse is surrounded by historic workboats and oyster sailboats at nearby docks, giving you the feeling that you have stepped back in time. The Hooper Strait Lighthouse, one of the three remaining screw-pile lighthouses in the Chesapeake Bay, is a cottage-type structure and one of the last of its kind.

For more information write to the Chesapeake Bay Maritime Museum, Box 636, Saint Michaels, MD 21663, or call (410) 745–2916.

© Mark Riddick/New Light Photography

COVE POINT LIGHT

Solomons, Maryland — 1828

For the better part of two centuries, mariners navigating the long middle reaches of Chesapeake Bay have watched for the powerful flash of Cove Point Lighthouse. At night the 150,000-candlepower light breaks over the dark waters of the bay every ten seconds.

The Cove Point beacon is so bright, in fact, that years ago a neighbor complained that the flashing light made it not just difficult but impossible for her to get any rest. Several times a minute, all night long, it blasted through her bedroom window, turning night into day. Apparently a lady of some influence, she demanded that something be done. To help her rest in peace, keepers hung an opaque curtain in the section of the lantern facing her house. As a result the Coast Guard *Light List* notes that the beacon is obscured from 040 to 110 degrees. Navigators who suddenly and mysteriously lose sight of the light on a dark Chesapeake night might find the explanation interesting.

Among the oldest lighthouses on the Chesapeake, Cove Point marks the entrance to the Patuxent River. The conical, 51-foot brick tower is the work of John Donohoo, a contractor from Havre de Grace. Donohoo also built the original Thomas Point tower and several other early Chesapeake lighthouses. The Cove Point Lighthouse was among his best, for it has stood intact since 1828.

Erosion threatened the structure almost from the day it was completed. By the 1840s keepers were reporting severe shore erosion, and retaining walls were built to hold back the bay, enabling the tower to survive at least another 150 years. Today the Chesapeake has cut to within a few feet of the old tower and may still claim its victim.

Although the light is now automated, Cove Point remains an active Coast Guard station and is off-limits to visitors. The area is easily accessible from nearby Solomons, Maryland, however, and the lighthouse can be viewed from the station fence.

HOW TO GET THERE: *Follow Maryland Highway 4 southeast from the Washington, D.C., Beltway to the town of Solomons. Here one can visit the Drum Point Lighthouse before proceeding to Cove Point. From Solomons take Cove Point Road to the Cove Point Coast Guard Station. Best viewing of the light is from about half an hour before sunset until just after dark. Helpful information may be obtained from the Calvert Marine Museum in Solomons at (301) 326–2042.*

THOMAS POINT SHOAL LIGHT

Chesapeake Bay, Maryland — 1825, 1838, AND 1875

The growth of shipping on the Chesapeake convinced the government to build a small tower on Thomas Point, not far from Annapolis. A bank of treacherous shoals extending out into the Chesapeake forced vessels requiring deep water to swing wide around the point. Obviously, a light was needed to help them keep their distance at night. In 1824 federal officials bought seven acres on the point for about $500 and hired a novice contractor named John Donohoo to construct a small tower for about $5,600. The inexperienced Donohoo did a poor job of building the tower, however, and a few years later, it had to be torn down and rebuilt.

The contract for reconstruction of the Thomas Point Lighthouse went to Winslow Lewis, who held a patent on the "reflecting and magnifying" lantern used in many American lighthouses (Lewis's system was eventually shown to be inadequate and was replaced in most lighthouses by high-quality Fresnel lenses). Lewis rebuilt the lighthouse for only about $2,500, and his tower guarded the point for more than thirty years. But its light was weak, and Chesapeake sailors grumbled that it was "utterly useless" in fog or foul weather.

In 1875 the Lighthouse Board decided to move the light offshore and place it where it would be most effective—out in the bay, immediately over the shoals. The new lighthouse was a small, hexagon-shaped building perched on screw piles. Abandoned, the Lewis tower on the point eventually collapsed, but for more than a century, the light on the shoals has weathered storms, floods, and ice floes—everything that nature has thrown at it.

The Thomas Point Shoal Light remains an active Coast Guard maritime beacon. However, the lighthouse itself is now managed and maintained by Maryland's Anne Arundel County, the Annapolis Maritime Museum, and the Chesapeake chapter of the U.S. Lighthouse Society. This unusual partnership of local government and private interest groups may have saved the historic structure, which is now the nation's last operational cottage-style lighthouse.

© Mark Riddick/New Light Photography

HOW TO GET THERE: *The only way to see this lighthouse is by boat. Annapolis, Maryland, is the nearest port. For possible sightseeing boat tours, contact the Tourism Council of Annapolis and Anne Arundel County, One Annapolis Street, Annapolis, MD 21401; (410) 280–0445.*

For more information on the lighthouse, write to the Thomas Point Shoal Lighthouse, P.O. Box 5940, Annapolis, MD 21403. To contact the Annapolis Maritime Museum, write to P.O. Box 3088, Annapolis, MD 21404, or call (410) 295–0140.

DRUM POINT LIGHTHOUSE
Solomons, Maryland — 1883

Many screw-pile lighthouses once stood in the shallow Chesapeake, but today only a few remain. One of these is Drum Point Lighthouse, a hexagonal, cottage-type lighthouse built on 10-inch, wrought-iron piles. Now part of a museum in Solomons, it once marked the north entrance of the Patuxent River.

Erected in 1883, the lighthouse cost $5,000 and took only about a month to build. Fitted with a fourth-order Fresnel lens, it showed a fixed red light, warning vessels of the sandy spit off the point. Having served for almost eight decades, Drum Point Lighthouse was taken out of active service in 1962.

HOW TO GET THERE: *Take Maryland Highway 4 south from Washington, D.C., to Solomons. The museum and lighthouse are on the left just before the bridge over the Patuxent River. The lighthouse has been wonderfully restored and furnished in early 1900s style. There is a small admission fee.*

The museum offers exhibits on the paleontology, estuarine biology, and maritime history of the region. For hours and additional information, contact the Calvert Marine Museum, Box 97, Solomons, MD; (410) 326–2042.

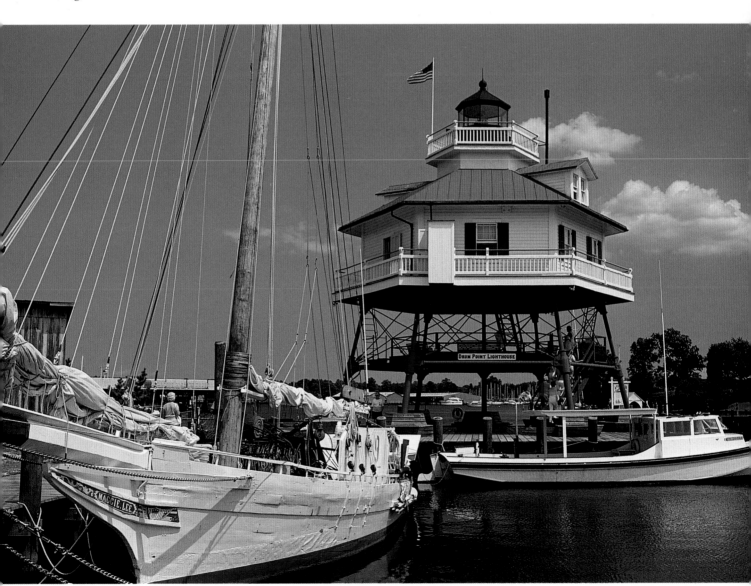

73

POINT LOOKOUT LIGHTHOUSE

St. Mary's City, Maryland — 1830

Strategically positioned between the Chesapeake Bay on the east and the mouth of the Potomac River on the west, the long, skinny finger of Point Lookout has been marked by a light since 1830. This was never a major light station, however. The $3,350 the Congress provided for the project proved sufficient only for a modest house with a small lantern perched on its roof.

This arrangement placed the light just 24 feet above the waters of the bay, and it could be seen from only a few miles away. While it helped ships avoid slamming into the point, it was otherwise of little use to navigators. Later the house was enlarged and the lantern raised to more than 40 feet, which considerably improved its range and usefulness.

The Coast Guard deactivated the station in 1966, replacing it with a more effective light on a nearby skeleton tower. The lighthouse is now part of Point Lookout State Park.

Navigators have often scratched their heads when they examine nautical charts of this part of the Chesapeake Bay. Not far from Point Lookout are Point Looking and Point No Point.

HOW TO GET THERE: *The lighthouse is located in Point Lookout State Park, at the very end of Maryland Highway 5, a few miles south of St. Mary's City. The park plans to restore the old lighthouse and open it to the public. The park itself is a wonder for anyone who loves water, as it affords a nearly 360-degree view of the blue Chesapeake. To contact Point Lookout State Park, call (301) 872–5688.*

Shirin Pagels

PINEY POINT LIGHTHOUSE
Valley Lee, Maryland — 1836

everal U.S. presidents, including James Madison, used Piney Point as a summer retreat. For this reason, some refer to the old light station here as the "lighthouse of the presidents." President Madison had come and gone for the last time, however, long before the lighthouse was built here in 1836.

A conical masonry cylinder only 35 feet tall, the Piney Point tower was built by John Donohoo for approximately $5,000. (Donohoo built many of Maryland's early lighthouses.)

In 1855 the station received a fourth-order Fresnel lens, making it the most prominent light on the Potomac. The light guided shipping traveling between Washington, D.C., and the open waters of the Chesapeake Bay. The light remained in operation for more than one and a quarter centuries before the Coast Guard deactivated it in 1964. The station now serves as a lighthouse museum.

HOW TO GET THERE: *The lighthouse is located off Piney Point Road several miles south of Valley Lee, Maryland. To reach Valley Lee, follow Maryland Highway 5 to Callaway and turn right onto Route 249. The Piney Point Lighthouse Museum, housed in a separate building near the Piney Point Lighthouse, depicts the story of lighthouses on the Potomac River. For hours and other information, contact the St. Clements Island–Potomac River Museum at (301) 769–2222.*

Assateague Lighthouse

CHAPTER FOUR

LIGHTS OF THE OLD DOMINION
Virginia

ROUGHLY A DOZEN YEARS after the Revolutionary War siege at Yorktown, the U.S. government built a lighthouse on Cape Henry, the very place where old Governor Spotswood of colonial Virginia had envisioned a tower and light a lifetime earlier (see page 2). Its fish-oil lamps were first lit one night in October 1792 and were still burning brightly some twenty years later, when British warships returned to the Chesapeake to fight the War of 1812. This time the Royal Navy met far less opposition at the capes than it had in 1781. In fact, the British captains may very well have used the Cape Henry beacon to help them steer their ships into the bay.

The invaders remained in the Chesapeake for more than a year, slamming the door on commerce and terrorizing the population. As the British burned and blasted one bayside community after another, the Americans fought back bravely but ineffectively with a pitiful array of clumsy barges on which they had mounted field cannon. At Hampton Roads the British captured Fort

Jones Point Lighthouse (© Mark Riddick/New Light Photography)

Monroe, using as a watchtower the Old Point Comfort Lighthouse, which had been in service for only about a dozen years.

Eventually, the redcoats attacked the City of Washington itself, setting fire to the Capitol and the White House. At Baltimore the British tried an unsuccessful military experiment, bombing Fort McHenry with rockets launched from small boats in the harbor. Most of the rockets exploded high in the air before they ever reached the fort. The British failed to capture the fort, but the sight of the rockets exploding like fireworks over Fort McHenry inspired Francis Scott Key to write a poem: "Oh say, can you see . . . "

IRON CLASHES WITH IRON

Almost a half a century after Key penned his famous lines, war again swept over the Chesapeake. This time it was a great Civil War, with American fighting American, North against South. Vastly inferior to the Northern side in naval strength, the Southerners were no friends of lighthouses. To make navigation as difficult as possible for Union sailors, the Confederates snuffed out all but a handful of the lights from Virginia all the way to the Mexican border. The Cape Henry Light was extinguished in 1861, the first year of the struggle. It remained dark in 1862, when the Confederates made their boldest attempt to punch a hole in the tight Union naval blockade of the Southern coasts.

On the morning of March 8, 1862, the Confederate States ship *Virginia* steamed out of the James River and bore down on a squadron of Union frigates anchored in the Chesapeake, within sight of the Old Point Comfort Lighthouse at Fort Monroe. Encased in a shell of iron plates 2 inches thick, the *Virginia* was a fighting ship such as the world had never seen.

Until this strange vessel appeared from around a bend in the James, sailors on the Union frigate *Cumberland* had been doing laundry and hanging their wet uniforms in the rigging to dry in the breeze. They had reason to be relaxed; as far as they knew, the South had no real navy. The last thing they expected was an attack, but incredibly, an attack was coming. There, in plain sight, was the *Virginia,* lumbering along at its sluggish top speed of five knots directly toward the *Cumberland*.

The laundry was snatched down out of the rigging, and the crew quickly readied the frigate's guns. The *Cumberland* started firing while the *Virginia* was still 3/4 mile away. But to their horror, the gunners on the doomed frigate saw their shots bounce harmlessly off the *Virginia's* thick armor. They reloaded and fired, reloaded and fired, but there was no stopping the *Virginia*. It kept plowing forward until, with a tremendous shock, it drove a 1,500-pound iron ram into the wooden ribs of the *Cumberland*. Mortally wounded, the Union ship went down swiftly, taking much of her crew with her.

That same day the *Virginia* also destroyed the frigate *Congress* and drove several other Union vessels aground on the spreading Chesapeake mudflats. Then, with night approaching, the Southerners took their seemingly invincible ship back to the James. But on the following day, they brought the *Virginia* out again, meaning to put an end to the Union blockade once and for all. This time, however, there was a surprise waiting for the Confederates. Directly in the path of the *Virginia* lay a low, turreted vessel described by one astonished Southern sailor as a "cheese box on a raft." But this small ship, its deck continuously washed over by the waves, was no joke. It was, in fact, an ironclad like the *Virginia*, part of a whole new class of fighting ships called "monitors."

The *Virginia* and the *Monitor* pounded away at one another for hours, but to little effect. Their historic confrontation ended in a draw. Neither would ever be defeated in battle, though within a few months both would be sunk. The *Virginia* was scuttled by its own crew to keep it from falling into the hands of Union troops who had overrun the Confederate naval yard at Norfolk. The *Monitor* sank in a fierce storm only a few miles south of the Hatteras Lighthouse.

U-BOATS OFF THE CAPES

The Civil War clash of the ironclads was not the last time that ships would fight near the Virginia capes. Many times between 1942 and 1945, the keepers of the Cape Henry Lighthouse saw flashes in the night and heard the thunder of exploding torpedoes fired by German submarines. Despite heavy patrolling by the Coast Guard and U.S. Navy destroyers, U-boat "wolf packs" often lurked in the waters beyond the capes.

The wolves were especially hungry during the winter and spring of 1942. On January 30 of that year, the tanker *Rochester* received a torpedo amidships and sank within sight of the Cape Henry

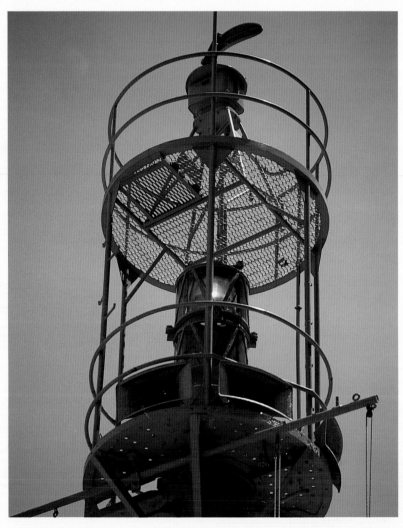

Light. Two weeks later a pair of torpedoes took down the tanker *E. H. Blum*, also near Cape Henry. On March 20 a German submarine sank the tanker *Oakmar*. In April the tankers *David Atwater* and *Tiger* and the freighters *Robin Hood* and *Alcoa Skipper* were all sent to the bottom by U-boats.

The carnage continued at intervals throughout World War II. The Cape Henry keepers would see a flash or hear a rumble and know that yet another vessel had fallen prey to the unseen enemy beneath the waves. There was little that the keepers could do but watch, lend lifesaving assistance if they could, and keep their lights burning.

The lantern atop the mast of the Lightship Portsmouth *guided countless thousands of mariners to the safety of the calm water in Chesapeake Bay.*

ASSATEAGUE ISLAND LIGHT

Assateague Island, Virginia — 1833 AND 1867

In 1831 Congress appropriated money for a lighthouse to be built a few miles south of the Maryland border on Assateague Island, about halfway between the Chesapeake and Delaware Bays. Its chief duty was to warn ships away from the dangerous shoals that extend from the Maryland and Virginia coasts like knife blades; however, after the light was completed and its lamps lit in January 1833, it proved too weak to perform this task effectively. But nothing was done about the problem for almost a quarter of a century.

Then, during the late 1850s, the Lighthouse Board launched a determined campaign aimed at repairing, upgrading, and correcting the many deficiencies of lighthouses all along the Southern coasts. As part of this comprehensive effort, the board decided to rebuild the Assateague Island tower. The Civil War interrupted the work, and the new lighthouse was not ready for service until October 1867. Once its lamps were lit, however, sailors could easily see the improvement. A first-order Fresnel lens made the light visible from 19 miles at sea.

The Assateague Island Light is now automated. It stands inside the Chincoteague National Wildlife Refuge, not far from the Assateague Island National Seashore.

HOW TO GET THERE: *To reach the Chincoteague National Wildlife Refuge from U.S. Highway 13 (the main road down the eastern shore of Virginia), take Virginia Highway 175 to Chincoteague; then follow signs to the refuge across the bridge to Assateague Island. Depending on the season, there may be a small admission fee to enter the wildlife area, which allows hunting. Call (757) 336–6122 for specific information.*

Although you can see the lighthouse as you cross the bridge to the island, the tower gets lost behind the trees when you reach the island. The person at the tollbooth can provide directions to the tower. A mile or so beyond the tollbooth is a large parking lot on the right-hand side of the paved road. From the park-

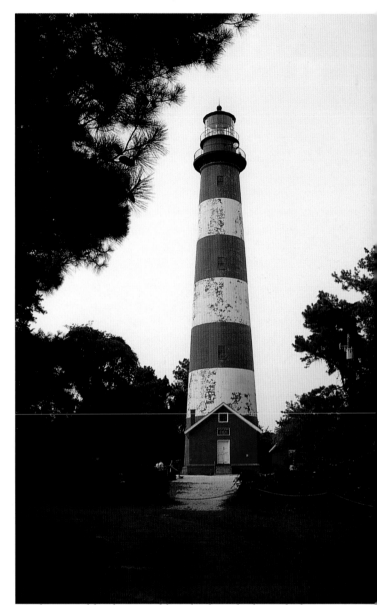

ing lot a trail leads several hundred yards through the woods to the lighthouse.

The tower is painted with red-and-white stripes and looks something like a candy cane without the curving top. A first-order Fresnel lens is on display near the base of the tower. The tower itself is closed to the public because the lighthouse is still in service.

Try going to the lighthouse in the late afternoon. If there are not too many other people in the area, you might see wild deer grazing about the tower as darkness falls.

CAPE CHARLES LIGHT

Chesapeake Bay, Virginia — 1828, 1864, AND 1894

Some thirty-five years after the Cape Henry Light began to guide ships into the Chesapeake, a second, smaller tower was built on the opposite lip of the bay. Completed in 1828 at a cost of just under $7,400, the 55-foot Cape Charles Lighthouse did little to improve navigation. Almost from the moment its lamps were lit, skippers complained that the light was hopelessly inadequate. Even under ideal conditions, the light carried only 12 miles; in heavy weather or fog, it could barely be seen at all. Even so, it remained in service for more than three decades before the Lighthouse Board thought of replacing it.

In 1858 the board launched construction of a 150-foot brick tower about a mile from the original Cape Charles Lighthouse. But, hampered by storms and shortages of materials, the work moved slowly. At the

outbreak of the Civil War, three years after the first brick was laid, the tower had reached only half its intended height. In 1862 a party of Confederate raiders attacked the construction site, driving off the work crew and destroying whatever they could. Another two years were needed to repair the damage and complete the tower. The lamps, which illuminated a first-order Fresnel lens, were finally lit on May 17, 1864.

As with many of the other Southern lighthouses, the nemesis of the Cape Charles Lighthouse has been erosion. In 1883 officials measured the rate of erosion on Cape Charles and discovered with alarm that the sea was moving 30 feet closer to the lighthouse each year.

Workers tried, but failed, to stop the advance with stone jetties. Then an engineering study revealed that halting the erosion would cost $150,000, a truly astounding sum at that time. So the board saw no alternative but to build another tower farther from the encroaching waves.

The new Cape Charles Lighthouse was begun in 1892 and completed two years later on a site roughly a mile inland from the original light station. The 191-foot tower is an iron cylinder only 9 feet wide, but it is reinforced by a pyramidal steel superstructure. The lantern is reached by means of a staircase inside the cylinder. Because of its design, unusual for a lighthouse located as far north as Virginia, the tower is strong but relatively light in weight. Since the members of the superstructure offer little resistance to the wind, lighthouses of similar design are often seen along the hurricane-plagued coasts of Florida and the Gulf of Mexico. Now automated, the Cape Charles Light remains in use.

HOW TO GET THERE: *Even the Coast Guard has trouble getting to this lighthouse. Located on a remote island near the northern lip of the Chesapeake Bay, it is not open to the public. The first-order Fresnel lens that served here until the station was automated in 1963 is now on display in the Newport News Mariners Museum; call (800) 581–7245.*

The **Lightship** **Portsmouth** *guided ships off the coasts of Virginia, Delaware, and Maryland. The crew's quarters, the galley, and the engine room look as if the crew is just on leave and could return at any moment to take the ship to sea. The beds are made, and the galley appears well stocked for the next meal. Photos and artifacts tell the story of life on a lightship during the early twentieth century. The museum is part of the Art Center complex on the Portsmouth waterfront. Contact the Lightship Museum at (757) 393-8741.*

LIGHTS OF THE JAMES RIVER
Newport News Middle Ground — 1891
Thimble Shoal — 1870 AND 1912

like the Delaware, Hudson, and Mississippi, Virginia's James River is not just historic, it is also vital to the economy of the region. The James provided America's earliest settlers with a convenient water highway to the interior. Now it does the same for ocean-going freighters and river barges. Also like the nation's other fabled rivers, the James is navigable only by way of narrow, winding channels broken here and there by deadly shoals. To make the river safer, dozens of lights were established along its banks or over open-water shallows. Over the years most of these were replaced by automated signals and other modern navigational devices.

Today only two important lights remain in operation on the James; both are near the river entrance at Hampton Roads, now one of the nation's busiest military and commercial harbors. One of these, the century-old **Newport News Middle Ground Light** lies far out near the center of the harbor. Built on an open-water caisson in 1891, it guards an L-shaped shoal that has claimed more than its share of off-course vessels. Shaped something like a coffee pot without a handle, the 35-foot cast-iron tower warns mariners with a flashing white light.

Also standing guard over Hampton Roads is the **Thimble Shoal Light,** a caisson-style structure built in

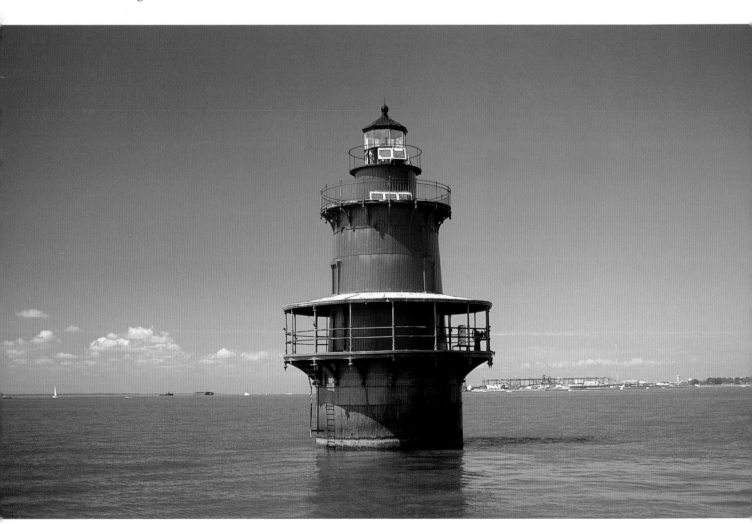

Middle Ground Light marks a dangerous shoal obstructing the busy shipping channels off Newport News, Virginia.

1912. A cottage-style screw-pile lighthouse placed here a few years after the Civil War was destroyed by fire in 1880. A second, similar lighthouse was frequently damaged by ships that strayed off course and slammed into it. The last collision came in 1998, when a coal scow hit the lighthouse and started a fire. The wooden tower burned to cinders. Set atop a 300-ton caisson, the existing cast-iron building proved far less vulnerable to collisions or fire, and it continues to guide harbor traffic after more than a century of service.

HOW TO GET THERE: *Both Newport News Middle Ground Light and Thimble Shoal Light are featured attractions of Hampton/Newport News harbor cruises. Call (757) 244–1040 or (757) 245–1533. On Museum Drive just off U.S. Highway 60 in Newport News is the excellent Mariner's Museum, which tells the story of humanity's long—and occasionally stormy—relationship to the sea. On display here is the huge first-order Fresnel lens from the Cape Charles Lighthouse; call (800) 581-7245.*

Like an image lifted from a Jules Verne novel, this strange-looking iron tower stands atop a massive caisson sunk directly over Thimble Shoal near Virginia's Old Point Comfort.

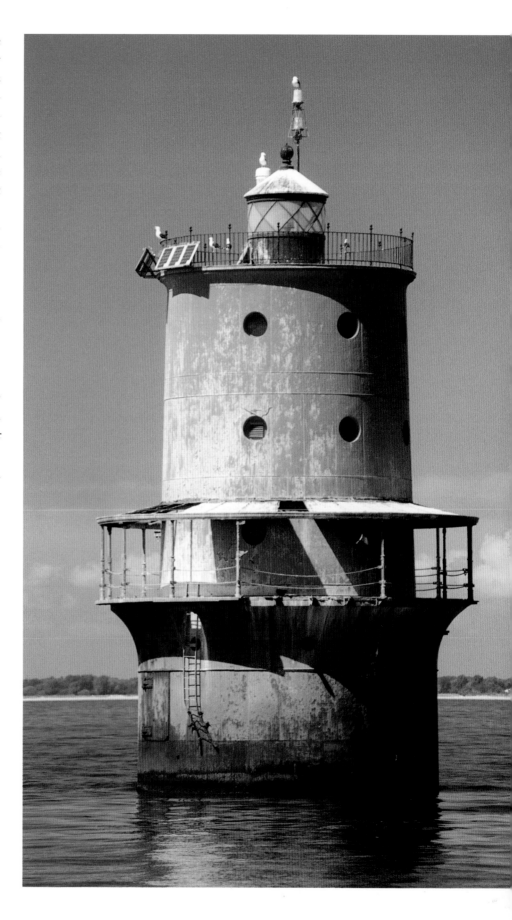

OLD POINT COMFORT LIGHT

Fort Monroe, Virginia — 1802

Among the earliest lighthouses constructed in the Chesapeake Bay itself was a stubby, 54-foot tower built in 1802 at Fort Monroe. The light marked the mouth of the James River and the entrance to Hampton Roads.

Because of its strategic location, the lighthouse saw plenty of conflicts; several crucial battles were fought within sight of the keepers in the lantern. During the War of 1812, British troops under Admiral Cockburn successfully stormed Fort Monroe and later used the lighthouse as a watchtower. Half a century later, the ironclad *Virginia* steamed past the Point Comfort Light on its way to do battle with the *Monitor*. Following the Civil War, Confederate president Jefferson Davis was imprisoned in a Fort Monroe cell not far from the tower.

Fort Monroe remains an active military post and is home of the Army Training Command. The lighthouse stands in the middle of Officers' Row.

HOW TO GET THERE: *To reach the fort drive west from Norfolk on I–64; then take the first exit after you emerge from the tunnel under Hampton Roads. The sentry at the Fort Monroe gate can provide directions to the lighthouse.*

The tower is not open to the public, but visitors are more than welcome at the Casement Museum, located a short distance from the lighthouse. A self-guided tour starting at the museum leads visitors through the historic fort.

Entrance to the fort and museum are free, and both are open daily. For more information contact the Casement Museum, P.O. Box 341, Fort Monroe, VA 23651; (757) 727–3391.

Old Point Comfort Lighthouse stands along Fort Monroe's Officers' Row (left). The 54-foot tower is still graced by the lovely fourth-order Fresnel lens installed during the 1850s (above). The Confederate ironclad Virginia *steamed past Old Point Comfort Light (right) on its way to battle the* Monitor.

NEW POINT COMFORT LIGHTHOUSE

Bavon, Virginia — 1804

The name *New* Point Comfort at first seems a misnomer, as it is, in fact, one of the oldest major lights in the United States. Built in 1804, it is very nearly the same age as the *Old* Point Comfort Light, completed in 1802 and located at Fort Monroe, about 2 dozen miles to the south. The 1804 lighthouse did not, as some mistakenly believe, replace the Old Point Comfort Light. Both lights are named after the separate Virginia headlands on which they stand guard, and these were likely given their names long ago by early Tidewater settlers.

In 1801 Congress appropriated $5,000—a handsome sum at the time—to establish a light station on New Point Comfort, at the entrance to Mobjack Bay. Government officials considered the expenditure justified, because the light would be of particular, strategic importance for shipping. Vessels steering to the west of the light would enter the York River, while those steering to the east and north were bound for the upper Chesapeake. The project took three years to complete, and the light entered service late in 1804. Elzie Burroughs, the station's first keeper, received his appointment from President Thomas Jefferson.

In 1852 the newly appointed Lighthouse Board sent inspection teams to examine thoroughly all the nation's navigational aids. At New Point Comfort, the inspectors found the half-century-old tower still in excellent condition. They reported that keeper Isaac Foster, a retired sea captain, maintained his light with the assistance of a female slave. The inspectors apparently saw nothing exceptional in this arrangement, but they did note that Foster received no allowance beyond his salary of $400 per year for the employment of his "assistant."

During the Civil War a Confederate raiding party attacked the lighthouse and knocked it out of operation. It was not repaired and relit until after the war ended in 1865.

Congress got very good value for its money. The 63-foot, octagonal sandstone tower still stands, virtually unchanged, after nearly two centuries. Unfortunately the station no longer serves navigators except as a day mark. Automated in 1919, it was finally decommissioned and abandoned during the 1950s. In 1981 Virginia's Mathews County restored the lighthouse as a memorial to local mariners who have lost their lives at sea.

HOW TO GET THERE: *Located on a small island surrounded by shallows and mudflats, the New Point Comfort Lighthouse can be reached only by boat. However, it is possible to view it from a boardwalk in the New Point Comfort Natural Area Preserve at the end of Route 600 in Bavon, Virginia. The preserve can be reached at (804) 725–4034.*

LIGHTHOUSES OF CAPE HENRY

Virginia Beach, Virginia — 1792 AND 1881

People talked about placing a lighthouse on Cape Henry, at the entrance to the Chesapeake Bay, a long time before anyone actually got around to building one. Among the numerous projects undertaken by Virginia's flamboyant Alexander Spotswood, who governed the colony for the British during the early 1700s, was the construction of a light tower at the mouth of the Chesapeake.

Every inch the cavalier, the governor was given to flights of romantic fancy; his ambitious proposals usually generated a great many toasts and a lot of high-toned conversation but not much action. For instance, in 1716 Spotswood decided to explore the unpopulated wilderness west of the Virginia tidewater, and he actually set off into the backcountry wearing a green-velvet riding suit and sporting a sweeping plume in his hat. Spotswood apparently saw his journey into the wilds as something of an extended foxhunt, since he took with him a dozen properly attired

Virginia gentlemen and a wagon creaking under a heavy load of wine and liquor. A few days after they had departed, Spotswood and his companions returned to their plantations in much too tipsy a condition to remember anything they had seen.

Spotswood could not interest the British government in his lighthouse idea, but the governor's proposal attracted numerous advocates in Virginia's House of Burgesses as well as among prominent planters and merchants throughout the Chesapeake region. Like the governor himself, however, they all found it far easier to raise a glass of port than to finance and construct a tall stone tower. Nearly half a century after Spotswood and his plumed hat had passed from the scene, the Cape Henry tower still had not been built.

In 1774 the colonies of Maryland and Virginia finally decided to move ahead with the project. Tons of stone were piled up at the construction site, but

"New" Cape Henry Lighthouse dates from 1881. It is seen here from the top of the Old Cape Henry tower, built in 1792.

New Cape Henry Lighthouse

Located at the entrance of Chesapeake Bay, Cape Henry can boast not one but two historic lighthouses. One of the first structures built by the U.S. government, the old stone tower on the left dates to 1792. Its black-and-white, cast-iron neighbor, completed in 1881, remains active.

funding ran out while the foundation was being laid. Before more money could be found, the drums of the Revolutionary War put a stop to the effort. After the war stonemasons understandably balked at working for worthless Continental dollars. So it was not until 1791, shortly after adoption of the Constitution and the establishment of a stable currency, that the project could continue. The nation's first federal Congress authorized a lighthouse for Cape Henry and appropriated $24,077 for its construction.

Contractor John McComb, hired by Secretary of the Treasury Alexander Hamilton, had at first hoped to use the stone stockpiled for the tower by colonial builders twenty years earlier. Unfortunately most of the big stones had sunk so deep into the sand that they could not be salvaged. Using freshly quarried sandstone, McComb completed the 90-foot tower in the fall of 1792.

McComb and his crews built a solid lighthouse; the tower has stood for two centuries, through several wars and countless gales. The Confederates put the light out of service briefly at the beginning of the Civil

War, but the Lighthouse Board had lamps burning again by 1863.

In 1870 a network of large cracks began to split the tower. Fearing that the lighthouse would crack open and collapse, the board had a cast-iron tower built about 100 yards to the southeast. Standing 156 feet tall, the new tower received a first-order Fresnel lens and began service to the Chesapeake shipping lanes on December 15, 1881. Both towers still stand today.

HOW TO GET THERE: *Both lighthouses are located on the grounds of Fort Story at the north end of Virginia Beach. To reach the fort, take U.S. Highway 60 south from Norfolk. The entrance to the fort, an active military post, is about 10 miles from downtown Norfolk. The guard at the gate will provide a car pass and directions to the lighthouse. A National Historic Landmark, the 1792 lighthouse is open to the public, and visitors may climb the 90-foot tower. The lighthouse is now managed and maintained by the Association for Preservation of Virginia Antiquities. For more information call (804) 422–9421.*

Montauk Point Light, Long Island, New York

INDEX

Numerals in italics indicate photograph/caption only.

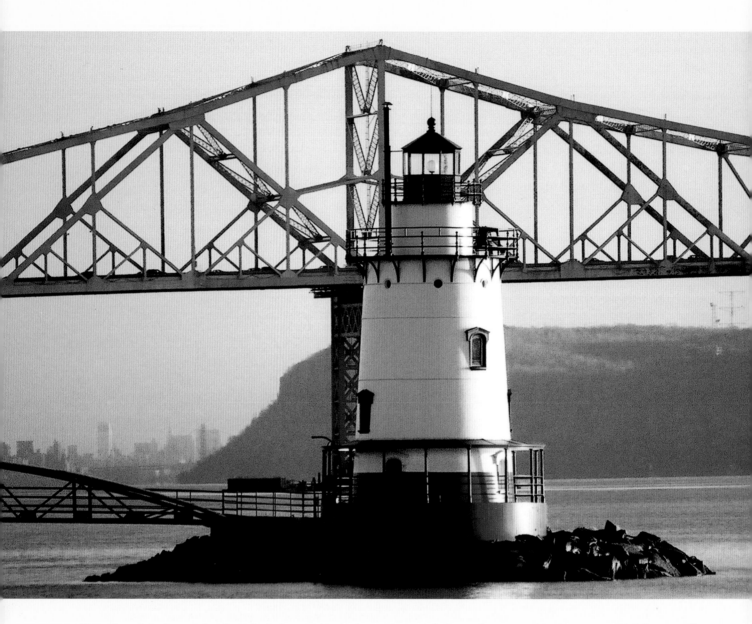

*Even though its lantern has been dark since 1961, the interesting sparkplug-style tower of the **Tarrytown Lighthouse** still stands. The old tower is part of Kingsland Point Park on the Hudson. (Shirin Pagels)*

ABOUT THE AUTHORS

BRUCE ROBERTS and his wife, Cheryl, who helped with the research for this book, live on North Carolina's Outer Banks, not far from the Bodie Island Lighthouse. For many years Bruce was senior travel photographer for *Southern Living* magazine. He started his career working as a photographer for newspapers in Tampa, Florida, and Charlotte, North Carolina. He is the recipient of many photography awards, and some of his photos are in the permanent collection of the Smithsonian Institution.

RAY JONES is a freelance writer and publishing consultant living in Pebble Beach, California. He began his writing career working as a reporter for weekly newspapers in Texas. He has served as an editor for Time-Life Books, as founding editor of *Albuquerque Living* magazine, as a senior editor and writing coach at *Southern Living* magazine, and as founder and publisher of Country Roads Press. Ray grew up in Macon, Georgia, where he was inspired by the writing of Ernest Hemingway and William Faulkner and worked his way through college as a disc jockey.

ALSO BY BRUCE ROBERTS AND RAY JONES

American Lighthouses
A Comprehensive Guide

Lighthouses of California
A Guidebook and Keepsake

Lighthouses of Florida
A Guidebook and Keepsake

Lighthouses of Massachusetts
A Guidebook and Keepsake

Lighthouses of Michigan
A Guidebook and Keepsake

Lighthouses of New York
A Guidebook and Keepsake

New England Lighthouses
Maine to Long Island Sound

Eastern Great Lakes Lighthouses
Ontario, Erie, and Huron

Western Great Lakes Lighthouses
Michigan and Superior

Gulf Coast Lighthouses
Florida Keys to the Rio Grande

Pacific Northwest Lighthouses
Oregon, Washington, Alaska, and British Columbia

Southern Lighthouses
Outer Banks to Cape Florida